Passementerie

Handcrafting
Contemporary
Trimmings,
Fringes,
Tassels,
and More

Elizabeth
Ashdown

SCHIFFER
CRAFT

4880 Lower Valley Road • Atglen, PA 19310

© 2024 Design and layout: BlueRed Press
© 2024 Text: Elizabeth Ashdown
© 2024 Photography: David Ashdown
© 2024 Lifestyle photography: Stephen Lenthall Photography

Library of Congress Control Number: 2023932559

All rights reserved. No part of this work may be reproduced or used in any form or by any means—graphic, electronic, or mechanical, including photocopying or information storage and retrieval systems—without written permission from the publisher.

The scanning, uploading, and distribution or this book or any part thereof via the Internet or any other means without the permission of the publisher is illegal and punishable by law. Please purchase only authorized editions and do not participate in or encourage the electronic piracy of copyrighted materials.

"Schiffer Craft" and the crane logo are registered trademarks of Schiffer Publishing, Ltd.

Produced by BlueRed Press Ltd. 2024
Designed by Insight Design Concepts Ltd.
Front cover design by Ashley Millhouse
Type set in Intervogue

ISBN: 978-0-7643-6718-2

Printed in China

Published by Schiffer Craft
An imprint of Schiffer Publishing, Ltd.
4880 Lower Valley Road
Atglen, PA 19310
Phone: (610) 593-1777; Fax: (610) 593-2002
Email: Info@schifferbooks.com
Web: www.schifferbooks.com

For our complete selection of fine books on this and related subjects please visit our website at www.schifferbooks.com. You may also write for a free catalog.

Schiffer Publishing's titles are available at special discounts for bulk purchases for sales promotions or premiums. Special editions, including personalized covers, corporate imprints, and excerpts, can be created in large quantities for special needs. For more information, contact the publisher.

We are always looking for people to write books on new and related subjects. If you have an idea for a book, please contact us at proposals@schifferbooks.com.

Other Schiffer Books on Related Subjects:

Macramé Couture: 17 Embellishment Projects, Gwenaël Petiot, ISBN 978-0-7643-5991-0

Artisan Felting: Wearable Art, Jenny Hill, ISBN 978-0-7643-5852-4

The Stuff: Upholstery, Fabric, Frame, Lorraine Osborne, ISBN 978-0-7643-6303-0

Abbreviations

DK	light, double knit weight yarn; CYC standard 3 light
DW	decorative weft
EPI	ends per inch
FW	fancy weft
FY	fringe yarn
MBW	main body weft
SW	structural weft

CONTENTS

INTRODUCTION	**4**

WHAT IS PASSEMENTERIE?	**8**
History of passementerie	12
How is passementerie used today?	16

GETTING STARTED	**18**
How to use this book	20
Materials and equipment	22
Yarn weights and sett	26
A guide to different yarn fibers	26
Selecting warp yarn	28
Working with color	29
Scallops and picots	30
Choosing decorative weft materials	31
Caring for passementerie	33
Weaving passementerie on a frame loom	34
Warping a rigid heddle loom	38
Winding shuttles and bobbins	45
Plying main body weft yarn	45
Plain weave	46
Weaving through the ground ends	50
How to use guide strings	52
Weaving with decorative weft	55
Removing weaving from the loom	57
Weaving in main body weft tails	58

TROUBLESHOOTING	**60**
Fixing a broken warp end	60
What to do if the decorative weft runs out	62
Common selvage problems	64

OFF-LOOM PASSEMENTERIE SKILLS	**66**
Tassel making using the embroidery skein method	66
Cord spinning	70
How to make fringe bunches	77
Square knot braid variation	79
Four-strand plaiting	82

PROJECTS	**84**
Bouclé fancy yarn cuffs for a jacket	87
Beaded tassel fringe for a lampshade	93
Dip-dyed Shetland wool fringe	101
Dahlia braid for a cushion	107
Scallop napkin rings	113
Cord-edged tassel cushion	119
Joséphine crête for a velvet cushion	123
Patchwork cuff bracelet	129
Wisteria border for a scarf	135
Margot crête fringe for a velvet footstool	141
Chromatic waves curtain tieback	149

GLOSSARY	**158**
RESOURCES AND SUPPLIERS	**159**
ACKNOWLEDGMENTS	**160**
ABOUT THE AUTHOR	**160**

INTRODUCTION

The mysterious world of handmade passementerie is a gloriously seductive art form. To an outsider, passementerie may seem like a mere frivolous decorative detail—the sort of thing you might find trimming a fusty old-fashioned set of curtains in a stately home. However, to those in the know, handmade passementerie is an exciting, diverse, and utterly contemporary art form that is rich in the very best of creative expression, luxury handcraftsmanship, and human ingenuity.

Passementerie creates the most spectacular visual feast for the eye, drawing you in with its sumptuously ornamental and decadent iconography. It is one of the rarest and most special of all the textile arts, and it is a craft that has been practiced around the world for centuries in many different forms.

Traditionally, the term "passementerie" describes the art of making small-scale yet highly decorative woven trimmings, ribbons, and braids, as well as handspun cords and handmade tassels, buttons, and rosettes, all of which are used to adorn and embellish grand interior schemes, furniture, hats, and garments. Since 2019, passementerie has been classed as an "endangered craft" in the UK, as there are so few professional makers working with the art form. At the time of writing, I am one of only six independent passementerie hand weavers working in Britain today.

My approach to passementerie is unique, and my distinct way of working with the art form has been described as iconoclastic,

The author. (Photo: Jeff Gilbert, 2023)

Sketchbook page showing passementerie designs, technical notes, and ideas.

INTRODUCTION

in the best possible way! With my work I am striving to keep this ancient art of passementerie alive, through making it relevant and exciting to modern-day living.

I have always loved textiles in all their various forms, and I have always been drawn to creative mediums that allow for the expansive exploration of color, pattern, and tactility. I have painted, knitted, macraméd, embroidered, and screen-printed, all in the pursuit of finding an art form that "clicked" with my brain. It was only when I was studying for a degree in textile design that I finally found an art form that suited the way my brain likes to work—weaving. For the last two years of my degree, I specialized in woven textile design—a glorious craft that combines technical skill, handcraftsmanship, color, and tactility.

I worked on projects designing furnishing fabrics, as well as fabrics for clothing, but it was only when I created a small collection of handwoven ribbons that I truly felt that I had found my form of weaving. The ribbons I made were nothing like the work I create now, but this initial body of work prompted me to research ribbon weaving, which in turn led me to stumble across the glorious and relatively unknown world of passementerie. As soon as I saw the fabulous array of decadent styles and techniques, I was immediately obsessed, and remain so still.

As a student, I taught myself how to create intricate and opulent handwoven designs by studying antique French weaving plates and sample books from the 1800s. I spent countless hours watching online videos about passementerie, just to discover glimmers of information about how these extraordinary textiles are created. Every weekend was spent combing through thrift stores and antique shops to find examples of handwoven designs that I could pick apart and study. I also realized just how much creative potential working on a small-scale offered. Furthermore, I came to realize that hardly anyone was working with passementerie in a contemporary way, and I felt that so much could be done with the techniques, skills, and materials of passementerie in a new and fresh way.

Close-up of a handwoven silk passementerie.

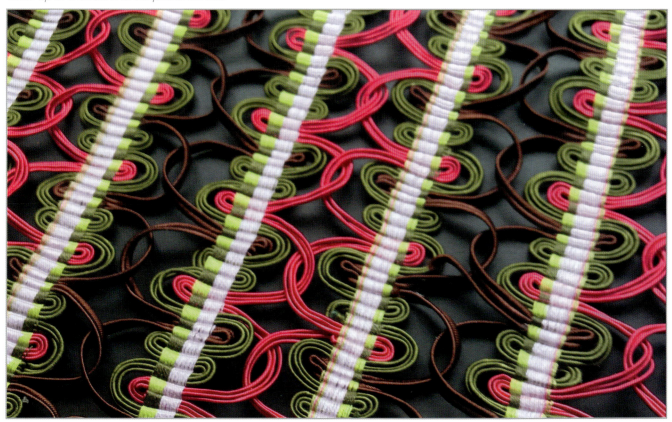

| 5

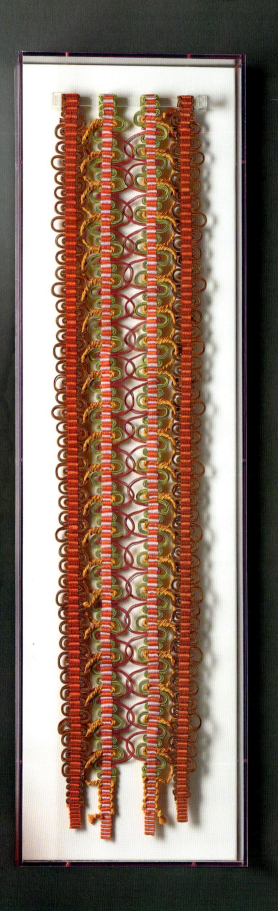

Until now, written instructions about how to make passementerie have been in very short supply. Most of my passementerie education has been developed through a lot of exploration, plus plenty of trial and error on my loom. Through exploration with techniques and weaving processes, I became able to work out how handwoven designs are made. Even now, the process and act of weaving a passementerie design is just as important to me as how the final design looks. I love taking individual yarns and materials and transforming them into extraordinary handwoven passementerie through processes as diverse as hand dyeing, cord spinning, looping, fringing, and scalloping.

After graduating from university, I worked as a freelance passementerie designer for interior designers and luxury interior-furnishing companies in the UK and Europe. A lot of my work at this stage focused on creating bespoke lengths of handwoven passementerie in traditional color palettes to coordinate with interior design schemes. I enjoyed this more commercial work; however, I was always being asked to create work that already existed—I felt that I wasn't ever adding something new to the world of passementerie. As an artist at heart, I was starting to feel stifled by the lack of creative expression within my work. So I made the radical decision to stop most of my commercial work in order to go back to university for two years to study for an MA in textiles at the Royal College of Art. This way I could thoroughly explore how to use passementerie in a completely new form.

Reinventing a centuries-old craft

During my MA I was able to radically transform my approach to passementerie by moving away from my more traditional and commercial work to a completely new, art-based practice. Today, as one of the last remaining craft passementerie artists, I use traditional hand passementerie skills to create to commission contemporary wall-based artworks that are full of intricacy, vivid color, and complex patterns. Through my practice, I am revitalizing this endangered craft by giving it a contemporary relevance. Passementerie is deeply rooted in tradition, and I feel that it is my role as a contemporary artist not only to respect this British heritage craft, but to move it on and develop it in new ways in order to appeal to modern sensibilities. I also

"Scottie" (2022). Handwoven passementerie artwork.

occasionally undertake commissions for bespoke lengths of passementerie if the project catches my eye! A lot of my work also focuses on highlighting this amazing craft to a much-wider audience, through curating exhibitions, writing articles, and teaching passementerie master classes online and in person.

I am very much inspired by antique examples of passementerie, and the style of work I create is heavily influenced by archival research. However, my work is not about historical re-creation, nor is it about heritage preservation for the sake of posterity. There are already passementerie creators who excel at this form of work. I am interested in creating a new future for the art form, and happily there is room within passementerie for all of us.

Materials and equipment

I have three essential tools for creating my passementerie—my looms, my cord spinner, and my hands. I have three shaft looms that I switch between depending on the project. My biggest loom is a floor loom called Big Bertha. Bought secondhand some years ago, Big Bertha is a four-shaft from the early 1970s. Originally used to weave rugs, Big Bertha is ideal for weaving large passementerie artworks, as the loom is very wide and really robust.

My cord spinner is an essential tool—I handspin around 95 percent of all the cords that I use within my artworks. I spin cords using fine silk in white or ecru. I then hand-dye all the cords, as well as hand-dyeing all the warps I use. This means that I can achieve very specific and bespoke colorways.

Making all my work by hand is extremely important to me.

I work in a wide range of sizes. My commissioned artworks vary in scale depending on the project—everything from 6 × 6 in. to 5 × 3 ft. I treat passementerie as if it is a component—each small individual warp is linked and joined together by hand on my loom to create a much-larger, connected textile.

My approach to color

Before I even decide what design I am going to weave, I spend a lot of time playing with color in my sketchbook. I am naturally drawn to bold and eccentric color combinations that work

Sketchbook showing ideas for passementerie artworks.

together to highlight, rather than fight, one another. I find that color is a very personal and instinctive component to work with, and I always begin a project by working with color spontaneously through drawing, coloring, and painting, before refining my ideas on the loom through creating lots of samples.

Find your own passementerie

One puzzling question I am often asked when someone is looking at one of my framed artworks is "What is this for?" Or more commonly, "What do I do with it?" I usually reply, "What do you do with your paintings?" Textile art has historically not been held in the same regard as other forms of artistic expression. This is particularly strong in the case of woven forms of textile art, including passementerie. However, whether used to trim a curtain or a cushion or when used as an artwork, passementerie brings tremendous joy to those of us who appreciate the artistry and craftsmanship that goes into making something by hand.

There is also a tremendous joy to be had in making your own passementerie designs: to create something extraordinary for you to enjoy in your home or within your wardrobe. While passementerie is steeped in tradition, I would encourage you to explore and play with passementerie to find your own version. My method is just one way of working with the art form. I've taught many students who have gone on to incorporate the techniques within ceramics, jewelry making, sculpture, and fine art. Find your own passementerie!

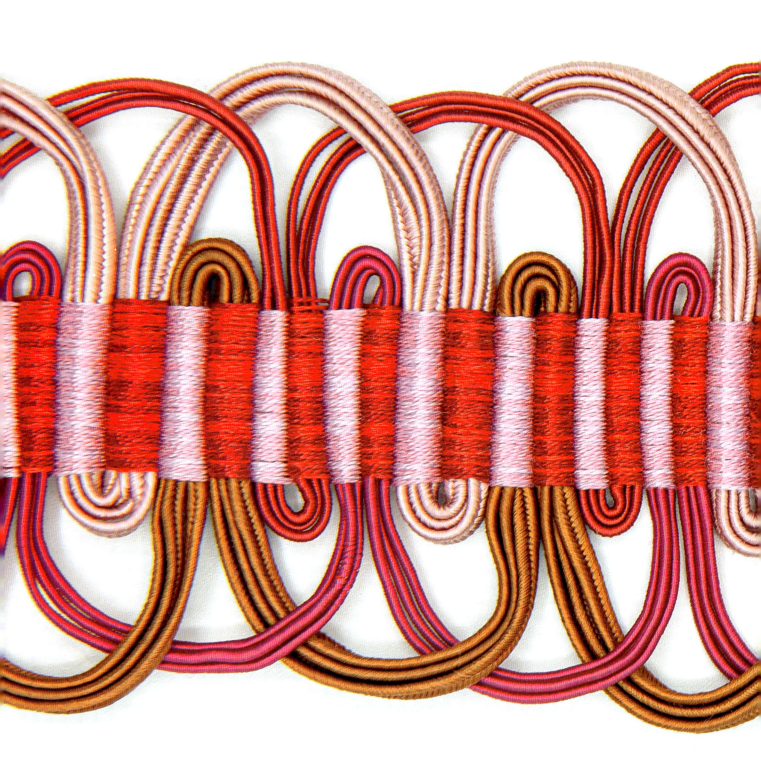

WHAT IS PASSEMENTERIE?

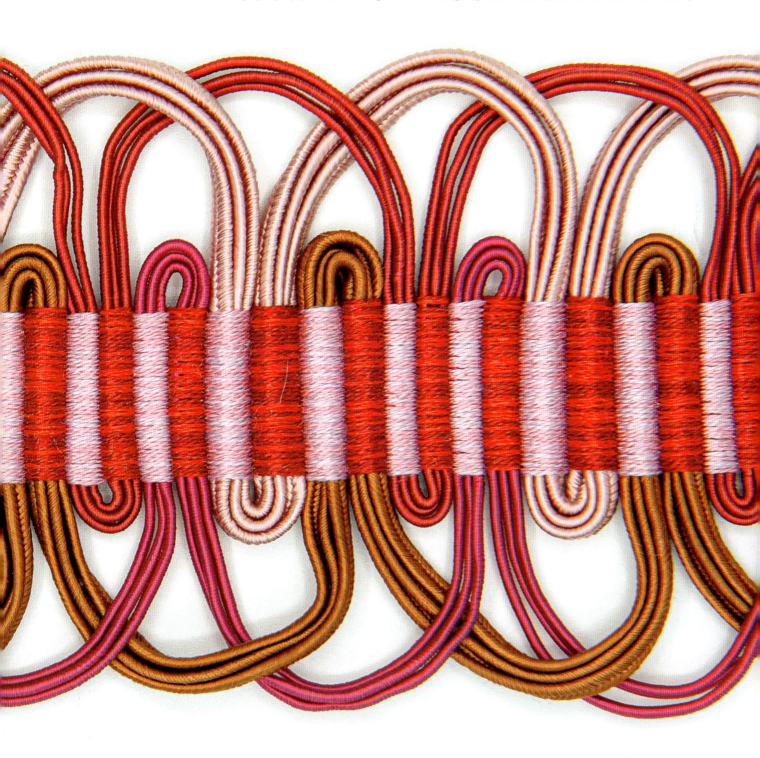

WHAT IS PASSEMENTERIE?

It is a mysterious, enigmatic, and underappreciated area of textile artistry. Steeped in a rich and diverse visual language, the names of passementerie designs are often just as intriguing as the designs themselves. Names such as Fly Fringe, Bullion, and Spangles intrigue with their otherworldly nature. The looms, equipment, and tools used to create handmade passementerie can also look just as curious as the textiles created through using them.

Passementerie creation combines the very best of human creativity and ingenuity, but what exactly is passementerie?

It is the art and craft of creating decorative and ornamental trimmings or edgings for interior design and fashion trimmings. The name "passementerie" originally stems from the French word *passement*, which refers to a type of gold or silver lace. Anecdotally, the name "passementerie" is said to have been developed from an expression translating as "turning of the hand," due to the intricate twists, turns, and loops that are the signature design elements of this art form.

Passementerie is an umbrella term for a vast range of different handmaking techniques, processes, and crafts. Broadly speaking, passementerie is split into three areas: weaving, cord spinning, and tassel and rosette making. The majority of passementerie lengths made today are woven—either by hand or by machine. Many woven passementerie designs cannot be made on an industrial loom, as this type of loom cannot rival both the complexity and beauty of what the human hand can create. Woven passementerie typically features a series of small and large loops that run up either side of a woven band. These loops are called scallops and picots. Woven passementerie can also incorporate many other textile techniques, including satin wrapping, pom-poms, and fringe making. Types of woven passementerie include braids, gimps, galloons, and crête.

Cord spinning and braiding is a vast area of passementerie creation. These techniques enable passementiers to create their own specific materials that are then used to create trimmings of all descriptions. In passementerie workshops, individual lengths

Handmade tassels by Samuel & Sons.

WHAT IS PASSEMENTERIE?

Robert Ely owns and operates Papilionaceous—one of the last remaining silk ribbon weavers in the UK. Robert crafts a wide assortment of striking designs for film and TV, costume, fashion, and art projects, as well as bespoke commissions.

of yarns are stretched out under tension in long rooms, before being spun or plied together to create all manner of cords that may then be woven into a braid or crête design or transformed into items such as hanging cords for elaborate tassels. Traditional wired gimp yarn is also created in a very similar manner.

Both rosettes and tassels are largely created by hand due to their intricate and multilayered nature. Rosettes, also called macarons, are traditionally used as decorative accents on the front of sofa arms and on the edges of bolster cushions. Tassels can be used in an infinite variety of ways, and there exist so many different iterations of tassels—everything from very traditional and ornate to thoroughly contemporary, rustic, and organic or glamorous—anything goes! A huge range of techniques and handmaking processes are required to create both rosettes and tassels. Techniques such as satin wrapping, ruff making, netting, macramé, and jasmin making all are required to produce these extraordinary objects.

Another area of passementerie creation is ribbon weaving and band weaving. Ribbons and bands differ in appearance to other types of woven passementerie as these items do not typically feature the intricate scallops and picots of other woven designs. Types of woven ribbons include petersham, grosgrain, and twill.

HISTORY OF PASSEMENTERIE

Ferrit, galon, gimp, tassel, and crête are just some of the evocative yet mysterious names of passementerie designs that have been produced by hand for centuries. However, rather intriguingly, the art of passementerie (also referred to as trimmings) is something of an enigma. For a craft that has been in constant production for centuries, very little written information exists, especially in regard to how designs are actually created. The secrets of how to create passementerie were typically passed from one generation to another through family-owned and family-operated businesses. Design information, dye recipes, and material suppliers all were closely guarded secrets. Very little information escaped these rarefied and mysterious workshops and ateliers, in order to keep passementerie creation in the hands of only a few privileged people.

Luxury passementerie workshops in Britain and Europe were patronized by wealthy members of royalty, the nobility, and the higher echelons of the church, all of whom choose to adorn their garments, castles, palaces, stately homes, and places of worship

Left: The Armada portrait of Queen Elizabeth I, showing her surrounded by passementerie of many kinds.

Right: Handmade rosettes by Samuel & Sons.

with the finest and most-glamorous examples of passementerie. This not only was to delight the eyes but was also a device to act as a sophisticated symbol of visual communication. The presence of passementerie in palaces and castles all over Europe not only created rich, captivating, and sumptuous interiors and fashion designs; these decorative accents provided an important function as crucial indicators of the owner's wealth, power, taste, and status in society. This may seem strange in our current age of fast fashion, where textiles are cheap to produce and acquire, but in previous centuries, textiles, especially passementerie, were commissioned, bought, and cared for as vitally important prized possessions.

The importance of passementerie in constructing and representing identity is illustrated to perfection in portraits of European aristocracy and royalty from the 1300s to the late 1700s. Individuals were painted wearing their finest and most expensive garments and posed against richly decorated textile backgrounds, dripping in the most luxurious and finest gold, red, and yellow trimmings, tassels, fringes, and laces imaginable.

Some of the most luxurious and glamorous passementerie can be found by walking in the footsteps of Marie Antoinette at the palace of Versailles. Here the staterooms and private apartments are richly adorned with some of the most exquisitely crafted passementerie ever created. The re-created designs are exact replicas of the passementerie selected by Marie Antoinette for her boudoir and private rooms. Made by hand in luscious silk shades of lavender, rose, and gold, this passementerie reveals the ultimate decorative visual spectacle that passementerie of all kinds can create. The latest fashionable garments at this time, especially evening dresses, would have similarly been festooned in all kinds of handmade passementerie, including delicate fly fringes, puffed trims, and narrow woven gimp braids.

While the term "passementerie" is French in origin, the act of adorning and trimming a living environment and clothing with decorative textiles and embellishments is a practice that is as

WHAT IS PASSEMENTERIE?

old as time. Every country and culture around the world has their own highly individual form of textile trimmings that are very close to the materials and techniques of passementerie as we know it today. Fragments of handwoven linen fringes have been found in ancient Egyptian burial sites, and items such as tassels and decorative knot work featured heavily for centuries as an important component of Japanese armor.

Passementerie designs past and present can be exceptionally ornate, opulent, and even ostentatious. However, it seems that the origins of the art of passementerie originally developed from a more functional need. Simple braids, handspun cords, and delicate fringes all were developed as a way of covering unsightly seams within upholstery in Britain and Europe. Nomadic tribes living in Asia and the Middle East combined form and function through their dazzling use of textile arts to create a form of trimmings that were both beautiful and useful to their needs, creating items such as heavily trimmed and decorated horse saddles and bridles festooned in colorful tassels and cords. In Europe, the art of passementerie quickly took off to focus on producing textiles of outstanding beauty and creativity. The increasingly elaborate designs created by artisans were used to adorn a room, or a garment, as if the textile were a fine piece of jewelry.

The term "passementerie" has been in use only since the seventeenth century in Britain. Before this time, a bewildering range of titles and names existed for the crafts involved in passementerie—at this point usually referred to collectively as "trimmings." Mysterious names such as "lace-man," "lace-woman," "fringe maker," "frog maker," "silkwoman," and "narrow weaving" all indicate the different roles played within trim creation, as well as the size and significance of the trimmings industry. Such was the popularity of passementerie in the time of Henry VIII that he employed several of his own dedicated trimmings makers at the Great Wardrobe to produce designs just for the Royal Household. These designs would have been made from real gold and silver, alongside silk and wool fibers dyed using the most expensive and prestigious natural dyes—red and yellow.

Passementerie by Samuel & Sons, featuring handmade tassels, cords, crête, and fringes.

WHAT IS PASSEMENTERIE?

The popularity of passementerie has waxed and waned as tastes in both fashion and interior design have changed across the centuries. Passementerie reached exuberant and extravagant heights in the Victorian era as the fashion for heavy, richly layered interior design schemes and fashions reached new heights. Almost every textile surface of a fashionable interior would have been covered in an assortment of richly ornamental tassels, bullion fringes, pom-poms, and trellis fringes. Luxury fashionable dresses, fashion accessories, and hats were similarly dripping in handmade trimmings of all descriptions.

Tastes in interior and fashion design rapidly changed during the Edwardian era, and these changes were further expedited by the dramatic social, political, and economic effects of the First and Second World Wars. In the intervening years, the trimmings industry in Britain gradually became eroded due to a combination of factors—design moved toward a minimalist aesthetic with the advent of modernism. Women's role in society altered dramatically, which in turn affected fashion choices, and many once-wealthy individuals stopped patronage of the luxury interior trades. All of this gradually led to the deterioration of a once-thriving industry, whittling the amount of trimmings companies down to a handful.

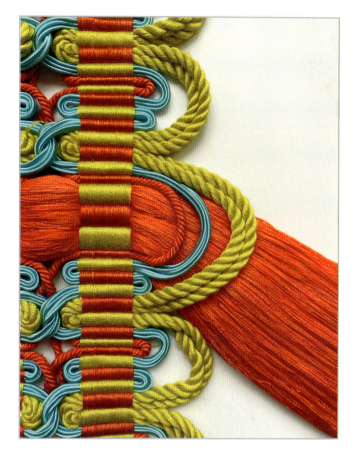

Above right: Handwoven passementerie artwork by Elizabeth Ashdown.
Right: Trim on an eighteenth-century dress.

| 15

WHAT IS PASSEMENTERIE?

HOW IS PASSEMENTERIE USED TODAY?

Passementerie is often referred to as "jewelry for the home," and today the popularity and interest in passementerie has exploded, especially among contemporary interior designers. The art is increasingly being used by these designers in an exciting, fresh, and innovative manner. Both handwoven and machine-made passementerie is used frequently in interior design, as an attention-grabbing, maximalist statement. While passementerie was traditionally used to trim a soft furnishing in a coordinating color palette, today designers are increasingly using passementerie as the soft furnishing itself!

The beauty of contemporary passementerie designs is that anything and everything is available today. There are no limitations or restrictions over designs, materials, patterns, or colors. Re-created classical designs from the 1700s sit beautifully alongside bright, colorful contemporary trims in a modern interior. Designs today can be elegant and soft, bold and flamboyant, or glamorous and lavish—there exists a design for every taste.

A renewed enthusiasm and appreciation for the handmade artistry of passementerie prevails, along with an interest both in preserving the heritage and traditions of the craft and continuing to revitalize the art in a new manner. Artists and designers are also drawing inspiration both from the aesthetics and making methods of passementerie in order to create a whole new manner and language for the art form.

The cornerstone of the majority of passementerie produced today is still very much rooted in classical designs and aesthetics from earlier centuries, but given a new lease of life through color, material, scale, and application. Passementerie companies and independent makers continue a generations-long lineage producing historical reproduction passementerie designs for a whole manner of palaces, historical homes, and both ceremonial military and royal accoutrements, most recently seen on fantastic display at King Charles's coronation.

A resurgence in popularity of costume drama movies and TV shows has also increased the demand for handmade passementerie of all iterations. Similarly, contemporary catwalk couture has taken a renewed interest in handmade passementerie, using the art form in increasingly opulent and fantastical ways as striking and dramatic statements. Increasingly, contemporary interior designers are using passementerie to create richly layered, bold, and energetic interior design schemes. Courtnay Tartt Elias at Creative Tonic uses passementerie with a playful and inventive flair to create sumptuous and joyful rooms.

I am very hopeful that the art and craft of passementerie is going to continue not only to survive, but to thrive for centuries to come. I believe that innovation and reinvention of the craft are constantly required in order to continue to make sure the aesthetics, forms, and making processes of passementerie continue into the future. However, this does not come at the detriment of more traditional and classical passementerie production—the beauty of this art is that there is room for everyone to thrive.

Interior designer Courtnay Tartt Elias of Creative Tonic Design creates luxurious layered environments that invite celebration. With a fearless use of color and a decidedly inventive flair, Courtnay designs stunning interiors that often feature an extensive use of passementerie. This is her Kips Bay Bar lounge.
(Photo: Stephen Karlish)

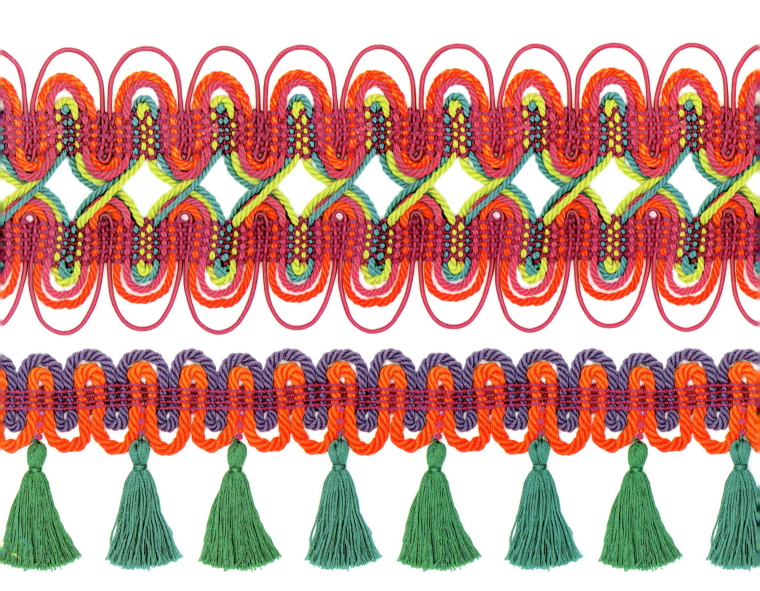

GETTING STARTED

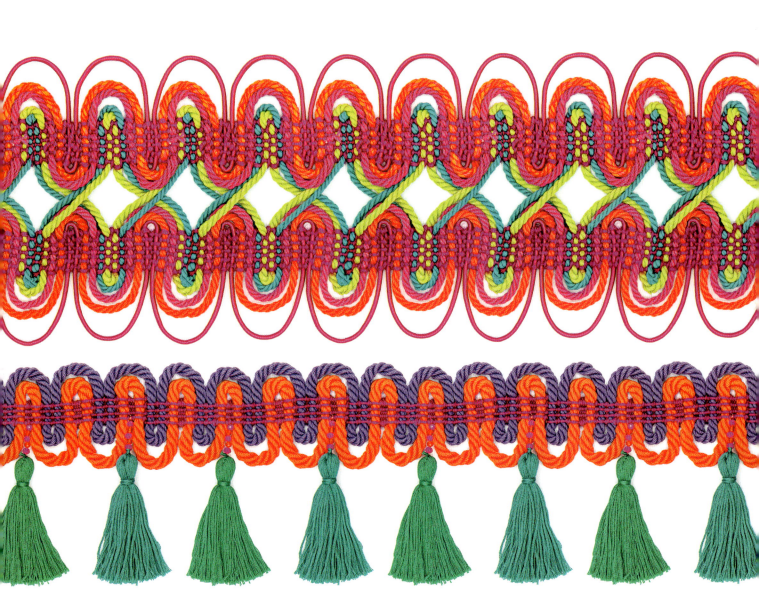

GETTING STARTED

HOW TO USE THIS BOOK

For this book, I have chosen to teach my favorite styles of passementerie that I use all the time in my own work. A lot of the designs are based on fabulous antique examples of French passementerie from the eighteenth and nineteenth centuries, but given a contemporary reinvention. I've made sure to include passementerie designs from the major passementerie categories, including fringe, braid, and crête. These projects should provide you with plenty of variety to adorn all manner of items in your home and wardrobe. I do hope the projects in this book will inspire and excite you to learn more about this fascinating and endangered craft.

Each project has step-by-step instructions as well as a comprehensive list of materials and equipment needed. When reading this book, don't be put off by the detailed instructions. Passementerie weaving can be complicated, but I have been careful to write the instructions as clearly and concisely as possible, while providing all the essential information required to make a project. After weaving a small amount of a design, you will quickly understand how the design repeats throughout its length, and your hands will quickly know what to do next, without having to follow my written instructions.

Make sure to read the instructions through before starting a project, and take special note of the different skills, materials, and equipment needed to make that particular design. Learn the projects in the order in which they appear, as the projects have been designed to build in complexity. Before you start a project, refer back to this "Getting Started" section to find instructions on how to set up your loom, ideas for working with color, and suggestions for how you can make your own cords for weaving.

Each project (except the dip-dyed fringe) demonstrates how to apply your finished passementerie to an item for your home or for wardrobe. These are just suggestions of how you could use your design—feel free to change the outcome as you wish. You may want to re-create a project exactly as it is shown here, but I really would encourage you to use the projects as inspiration to create your own original passementerie work. For example, you may like to experiment with different types of decorative weft rather than the suggestions I have made, or you may want to weave a design at a much smaller scale than I have suggested. Passementerie needs to be continually reinvented in order to ensure that this endangered craft survives and thrives, so do feel free to put your own unique spin on my designs.

Looms and weaving knowledge

Don't worry if you are a novice weaver or a weaver who has not woven for a long time. You will find comprehensive instructions for each step of the weaving process in this book. All the projects have been written for weaving passementerie by using a rigid heddle loom. I chose to use this type of loom for a number of reasons: it is a simple and accessible way to weave, the loom can be set up quickly, the loom takes up little space, and the weaver does not need to know about the technical intricacies of weaving in order to be able to use it effectively.

Choosing a rigid heddle loom

There are many different types of rigid heddle loom available, depending on your needs. All the projects in this book have been woven using the 16 in. (40 cm) Ashford Rigid Heddle Loom, which can be used on a table, or a separate stand can be purchased for the loom to sit on. If you can, I would strongly encourage you to visit a loom store in person before you buy one.

Rigid heddle loom vs. a shaft loom

In order to create my own work, I use a shaft loom. I use two different looms for my weaving: an eight-shaft table loom and a four-shaft floor loom—both of which work in the same way. A shaft loom works in a different way from a rigid heddle loom, and because of this, my shaft-loom passementerie looks slightly different from that woven on a rigid heddle loom.

Transferring designs to a different type of loom

Each of the designs in this book can be woven on any type of loom, including table, floor, inkle, frame, and even backstop looms. The beauty of weaving passementerie is that the designs are not reliant on using a particular type of loom.

HOW TO USE THIS BOOK

If you are using a different type of loom other than a rigid heddle loom, you will need to adjust certain aspects, such as warp yarn selection, loom setup, and warp setup, according to the type of loom you are using. The actual weaving of the passementerie design in terms of configuration remains the same. Please see page 34 to learn how to use a frame loom for passementerie weaving.

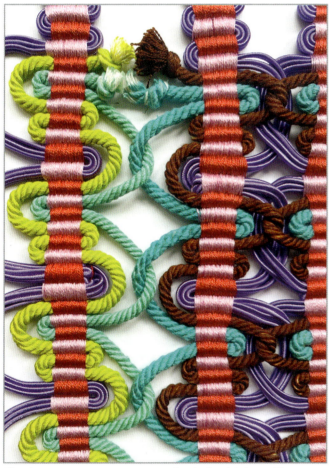

This design was woven using my eight-shaft table loom. The warp runs vertically up the photo. A shaft loom enables me to create a very dense warp. None of the decorative wefts are visible through the warp. This type of weaving is called "warp faced."

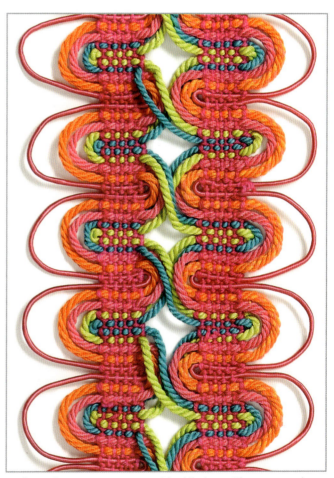

A design being woven on a rigid heddle loom. The warp on this type of loom cannot be made dense, which results in a design where the decorative wefts are visible through the warp. This type of weaving is called "weft-faced."

GETTING STARTED

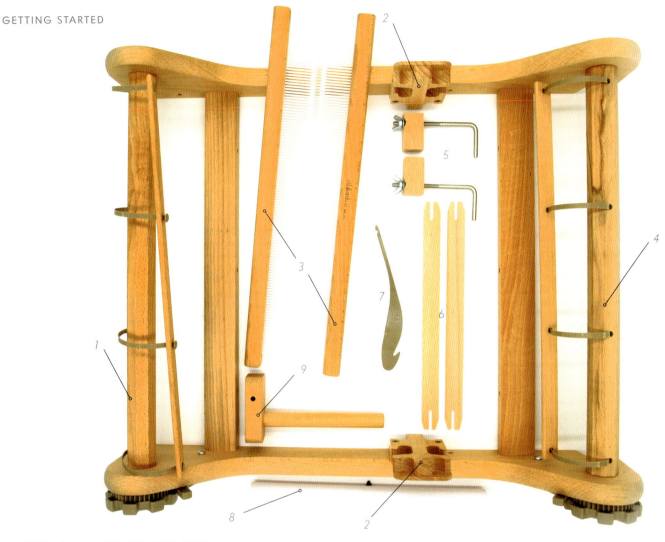

MATERIALS AND EQUIPMENT

Described here is the essential equipment you will need to hand-weave your own beautiful passementerie designs. Very little specialist equipment is needed, as most of the tools are ones you will easily find in any good weaving-supply store. If you are a weaver already, you most likely have all the tools and equipment you need to get started.

The rigid heddle loom

All the projects in this book have been woven using a 16 in. (40 cm) wide Ashford Rigid Heddle Loom. This loom comes with all the equipment and tools you will need to get started. The rigid heddle loom is ideal both for novice passementerie weavers and novice weavers generally. This type of loom is very quick and easy to set up and use.

1. **Back roller / beam and back roller / beam stick** The warp yarn is secured around the back roller / beam stick and then is rolled around the back roller/beam.
2. **Reed support blocks** are where the reed is positioned.
3. **The reed** has eyes and slots that the warp yarns are passed through. The reed is also used as a beater to push the rows of weaving into place.
4. **Front roller / beam and front roller / beam stick** The warp yarn is tied to the front roller / beam stick. The completed sections of weaving are gradually rolled around the front roller / beam as the weaving progresses.

Warping tools and equipment

5. **Clamps:** For securing the loom in place when putting a warp on the loom.
6. **Shuttle sticks:** For carrying the main body weft yarn through the warp.
7. **Threading and reeding hook:** A multipurpose tool used for both threading and reeding the warp yarns.
8. **Warp paper:** Your loom may be supplied with cardboard warp sticks. I prefer to use sheets of regular letter-size printing paper to create a layer of separation between the warp when it is wound around the back beam / roller of the loom.
9. **Warping peg:** Used for creating a warp.

Rigid heddle loom reeds

The reed is used to divide the warp yarn evenly across the front of the loom. The terms *reed* and *rigid heddle* can be used interchangeably.

The reed sits inside the reed support blocks, and the warp is threaded through the reed; this is also called *sleying* the reed. The reed has gaps in between each plastic intersection. These gaps hold the warp yarn. The collective name for these gaps is dents.

There are two types of specific gap in the reed—the slots and the eyes.

1. Reed spacing size number.
2. Eyes.
3. Slots.

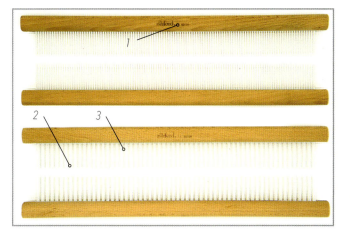

The slots are open channels that run vertically from the top to the bottom of the reed. One warp yarn is placed in one slot.

The eyes are small openings that sit at the halfway point within the reed. One warp yarn is placed in one eye.

When the warp is completely set up and you are ready to weave, the reed is raised and then lowered per row of weaving in order to create the shed. The warp yarns threaded through the slots and eyes in the reed are alternately raised and lowered due to the configuration of the slots and eyes.

Selecting a reed for passementerie weaving

Your rigid heddle loom may have come with a reed when you purchased it. However, this reed may be unsuitable for passementerie weaving, as the density of the reed may be too open and gappy.

A reed for a rigid heddle loom provides a variety of functions to the weaver:
- Acts as a beater to compress the rows of weaving.
- Creates the shed in the warp.
- Divides a warp evenly across the loom.
- Maintains the desired warp width and sett (see below).
- Prevents twists and tangles in the warp.

It is very important to select the right reed for a project, as selecting the wrong one can cause significant problems during the weaving.

How do I choose the right reed for my project?

All the projects in this book have been woven using a number 15 epi reed, also called a 60/10 cm reed. This means that to a 1 in. horizontal space in the reed, there are 15 dents. Or to a 10 cm horizontal space, there are 60 empty dents.

This reed has been selected to weave the projects in this book, as it provides the optimal number of dents to weave passementerie, using a double-knit (DK) weight yarn as the warp.

Reeds are available in a variety of dent densities, and the appropriate density is selected based on the weight of warp yarn that is being used to weave a project. For example, if a

GETTING STARTED

chunky yarn is used as a warp yarn, a very open-density reed would be used (e.g., 2.5 epi or 10/10 cm). If a finer yarn is used as a warp yarn, a denser reed (e.g., 15 epi or 60/10 cm) would be used.

Why do reeds vary in density?
Every type of yarn has something called the sett. This refers to the number of warp yarns (ends) that a yarn needs to have per inch of warp in order to weave correctly. This is also called ends per inch or epi.

Every different weight of yarn has its own epi. For example, a DK yarn typically has an epi of 15. This means that the yarn needs to have 15 individual warp yarns to an inch space on the loom. This ensures that the warp yarn weaves at the correct density. A very chunky wool yarn may have an epi of 4. This means that the warp needs to have only four individual warp yarns to a 1 in. space on the loom in order to weave correctly.

The reed you select for a project is based on the warp yarn's epi. Taking the example above, a DK wool yarn has a sett of 15 epi. This means that a 15 epi or 60/10 cm reed needs to be used to give an overall finished warp set of 15 epi when the reed is threaded. As all the projects are woven in this book by using a DK wool warp yarn, only a 15 epi / 60/10 cm needs to be purchased.

What if I used the wrong density of reed?
If you were using a DK wool warp yarn with a sett of 15 epi and you used a 4 epi reed, the resulting woven passementerie would be too open and loosely woven. There would be huge spaces between the warp yarn in the dents of the reed. This would create a textile that is not stable enough to be used once removed from the loom.

Conversely, if you used a chunky wool warp yarn with a sett of 4 epi in a 15 epi reed, the warp would be unusable as there are too many warp yarns crammed within a 1 in. space.

Frame loom equipment and tools
Pictured above is the Rico large frame loom, measuring 12 × 15.5 in. (30 × 39.5 cm). Frame looms come in many different sizes. Passementerie can easily be woven using a frame loom, and all the designs featured in this book can be woven using a frame loom. However, the disadvantage of using a frame loom is that the length of passementerie you can weave is severely restricted.

1. **Frame support bar.**
2. **Metal fork** Used as a beater to push the rows of weaving into place
3. **Yarn shuttles:** One shuttle is used to carry the main body weft yarn through the weaving. The second shuttle is used as a shed stick. Frame looms usually come with medium- to long-length shuttles. For passementerie weaving, you might like to purchase shorter stick shuttles (see the following pages).
4. **Notched frame loom**: The notches hold the warp yarn in place. This frame loom has four notches to 1 in.

MATERIALS AND EQUIPMENT

Other materials and equipment

1. Dressmaking pins.
2. Regular sharps needle and blunt-end wool needle.
3. **Snap bobbin:** These come in various sizes. Yarn or decorative weft can be wrapped around the bobbin, which is then snapped shut to hold the yarn in place. Length can be pulled through without having to unsnap the bobbin. A handy way of keeping yarn contained and so preventing tangles.
4. **8 in. (20 cm) small boat shuttle:** Alternative to a stick shuttle. Used for carrying the main body weft yarn through the warp. As passementerie weaving is very narrow, it is much easier to use a small boat shuttle.
5. **6 in. (15 cm) small stick shuttle:** For carrying the main body weft yarn through the warp. As passementerie weaving is very narrow, it is much easier to use a small stick shuttle. It is good practice to have two stick shuttles to use.

Note on shuttles: Choosing the right type of shuttle is fairly subjective. I used both a stick shuttle and a boat shuttle to weave the projects in this book. Try both and see which you prefer.

| 25

GETTING STARTED

YARN WEIGHTS AND SETT

Guide to different weights of yarn

Choosing a beautiful yarn to weave with is one of the most exciting parts of starting a new passementerie project. There are so many different yarns available in a bewildering range of textures, fibers, colors, and weights—sometimes it can be tricky to work out which yarn to buy for a project.

All the step-by-step projects in this book have been written for using a 100 percent wool light/DK yarn for the warp yarn. Some of the projects use different weights and textures of yarn for the main body weft.

If you are an experienced weaver who understands the technicalities of choosing different warp yarns, yarn sett, and ends per inch, I would encourage you to experiment with different weights of warp yarn when you have completed a few of the projects using DK yarn.

If you are a novice weaver, or you don't have much weaving experience, I would encourage you to stick to using 100 percent wool DK yarn for the warp yarn. As your confidence and knowledge grows, feel free to experiment with different types of main body weft yarn in different textures and fibers. Just changing the main body weft yarn, but keeping the warp yarn the same, can have a dramatic effect on the overall look of your design.

What is a yarn weight?

Yarn comes in different weights; these refer to the thickness of the yarn and not how much the yarn actually weighs. Each different type of yarn fiber (e.g., wool, silk, cotton, and linen) has a different weight-counting system, and this can be very confusing and technical to understand! As all the projects in this book have been written to use readily available knitting yarns, I have given a simple explanation of the yarn weights that you will commonly come across. Note that the names given may vary depending on the country you live in.

Common yarn names	Yarn ply	Description
Lace/thread/fingering/cobweb	2 ply	Very fine yarn
Superfine / sock weight / baby	3 ply	Lightweight yarn, roughly half thickness of DK yarn
Fine/sport/baby	4 ply	Thin yarn
Light / double knit	8 ply	Medium-weight yarn
Medium/aran/worsted	10 ply	Medium to chunky yarn
Bulky/chunky	12–14 ply	Thick weight
Super bulky/super chunky/jumbo	16 ply +	Very thick yarn

A GUIDE TO DIFFERENT YARN FIBERS

So many exciting fiber combinations exist in yarns. One of the things I love about contemporary passementerie is that it can have such a broad range of aesthetics and qualities, depending on the fibers chosen to weave the design. The fiber used will dramatically affect the finished passementerie's drape, softness, texture, feel, weight, and flexibility. The best way to explore different fibers and yarns is to create a collection of small passementerie samples woven in different materials. You can then use this as an inspiration library to design longer lengths of passementerie.

All the projects in this book use 100 percent smooth wool as a warp yarn. Some of the projects use a strong and smooth wool

and silk combined yarn. Both these yarns are very strong and are very easy to work with. They also give a lovely handle once the passementerie is removed from the loom.

Natural fibers. This is yarn made from plant fibers or animal fleece/hair (e.g., wool, silk, cashmere, and mohair). It is very common to find multiple natural fibers blended into one yarn (e.g., silk and cotton mix). For most purposes I prefer to use natural fibers to weave with, as I feel that they give a much nicer, more refined final result. Additionally, natural fibers are often much nicer to handle when weaving—an important consideration when hand-weaving passementerie.

A GUIDE TO DIFFERENT YARN FIBERS

Synthetic fibers These yarns are made from chemical processes (e.g., polyester, acrylic, and nylon). Be careful if selecting synthetic fibers, as they often require an experienced hand to work with them effectively. Typically, they are slippery, smooth, and shiny yarns that can often cause difficulties when used as main body weft or warp. Synthetic yarns such as Lurex or metallic threads can often make beautiful fringes, especially when plied with a natural fiber for stability.

Fiber type	Description
Wool	The classic fiber for yarn. It has been used to create passementerie for centuries, although its use is not as popular in contemporary commercial passementerie designs. Wool can add a lovely textural quality. It comes in a huge variety of different qualities and textures—everything from supersoft and delicate to chunky and scratchy.
Blended yarn / plied yarn	Yarn made from multiple strands of yarn spun into one length. Can be made from one type of yarn, or different types of fiber can be plied together to create one yarn.
Superwash wool yarn	A wool yarn that has been specially treated to make it safe for machine washing. As I would not generally recommend putting passementerie through the washing machine, this is not an important yarn to use, except if weaving more practical designs for fashion.
Silk	A classic yarn used time and again in passementerie weaving. It is the quintessential luxury yarn, available in a huge range of textures, colors, and weights. Silk has a beautiful drape and handle. It can be very difficult (and expensive) to find a thicker silk yarn that is suitable to use as a warp for a rigid heddle loom. Silk makes a beautiful handwoven fringe and looks exquisite spun into a cord. A silk and wool blend DK yarn is ideal to use as a warp yarn, provided the yarn is smooth and nontextured.

Cotton, linen, bamboo	These yarns make great alternatives to using animal fibers. The drape, look, and handle of these fibers will behave differently in comparison to animal fibers. Extra care must be taken over yarn selection if using one of them as a substitute for DK wool yarn as warp. If you are not an experienced weaver, these fibers are best kept for main body weft.
Mohair	Best used for main body weft and cord spinning. Mohair is an excellent yarn for creating a soft, hazy effect in your weaving. However, don't use as a warp, as it is extremely difficult to work with.
Merino	A thinner and softer type of wool, merino provides a less textured and smoother surface. Typically thinner than DK yarn, merino is best kept as main body weft.
Nylon	Man-made synthetic fiber extracted from crude oil. Don't use nylon yarn on its own, as it won't give you an appealing quality or handle. Nylon is often blended into other yarns in small amounts to give strength to other fibers.
Polyester	Plastic-based, man-made synthetic fiber. Best avoided in passementerie weaving.
Lurex	A shimmering metallic yarn that can make excellent handwoven fringes. Lurex is made from aluminum and plastic film. Quite often found in ready-made cords available in haberdashery shops.
Eco and recycled yarns	Lots of recycled yarn options exist (e.g., cotton yarn made from recycled denim, T-shirt yarn). Be careful of strength if using as warp. Best kept for main body weft or cord spinning.
Handspun yarn / art yarn	Unique yarn that has been made by hand, using either a drop spindle or a spinning wheel. Handspun/art yarn is often uneven in texture, which makes it so special and beautiful. For this reason it is best kept for main body weft or cord spinning only.

GETTING STARTED

SELECTING WARP YARN

Traditionally, passementerie has been woven on a shaft floor loom using incredibly fine warp yarns, using a special weaving technique called "warp rib." This creates a very dense, crammed woven surface. Typically, passementerie has been woven from shiny yarns such as silk, viscose, mercerized cotton, and synthetic yarns. These yarns, in combination with warp rib, create the signature passementerie look. This warp rib appearance is almost impossible to achieve using a rigid heddle loom or a frame loom. Due to the nature of how these looms work, sufficient yarns cannot be "crammed" in the warp. It is also very difficult to use fine warp yarns on these types of loom. However, using a rigid heddle loom or a frame loom offers so much potential to create a thoroughly fresh and contemporary spin on traditional passementerie through using nontraditional yarns and materials.

A enormous amount of yarn is available to purchase, and it can be very hard to know where to begin when it comes to selecting an appropriate warp yarn to use. The choice depends on many factors, such as how the weaving will be used (e.g., durability, warmth), design decisions (color, texture), the skill level of the weaver, thickness, and drape, to name just a few considerations.

All the projects in this book have been designed to use 100 percent DK wool yarn as a warp. This is for a few reasons: this yarn suits the workings of a rigid heddle loom perfectly. It is generally strong, smooth, well behaved, and easy to work with. It does not snap, fray, stretch, or unravel easily. It is also an accessible yarn to use because it is available in a limitless range of wool compositions, colors, and price points. You will easily be able to source a range of exciting 100 percent wool DK yarn from any knitting-supply store.

Warp strength test

Choosing the right yarn for a warp can make or break a weaving project. Selecting a smooth, strong, and well-behaved yarn will minimize the risk of warp problems, such as unraveling, fraying, stretching, or snapping.

If a 100 percent wool DK yarn is highly textured, slubby, knotted, or loosely spun, then it is not suitable for a warp, as any textures, twists, etc. in the yarn will cause problems once on the loom.

The warp yarn is held on the loom under a lot of tension, so it is essential to select a yarn that can withstand this tension for long periods of time:

To test the strength of a proposed warp yarn, unravel a length of yarn from the ball. Clasp either end of the yarn between thumb and finger. Pull tightly on the yarn. If it breaks easily, unravels, or starts to fray, it is not suitable for a warp yarn. If it does not break, it is suitable.

Test fluff level

Yarns that "fluff up" easily will cause problems if used in the warp. The warp is constantly being raised and lowered to create the shed, which causes the warp yarns to rub together. If the warp yarn cannot stand the abrasion of the shed, it will start to fluff up. These fluffed-up areas will then catch on the warp yarns surrounding the fluff, causing the weaver a large headache!

Unravel a length of yarn and fold it back on itself. Between your fingers, vigorously rub the yarn so the two lengths rub together. If there is any sign of them becoming fluffy, this yarn is not suitable to be used as a warp.

WORKING WITH COLOR

Color is my most important tool, as it offers exciting and limitless possibilities within passementerie weaving. In my own work, I favor strong, bold, and energetic color palettes where each individual color works together to make its neighbor appear even more zingy and full of life. Color is a fascinating tool to work with, and the way in which it is used can easily make or break a design. Color is also very subjective—I love saturated color palettes because they make me feel happy, whereas a quieter and more subtle palette may bring you joy. Both will work equally well in passementerie.

Passementerie is typically woven to accent an interior design scheme, rather than being used as a bold, statement piece. So a lot of commercial passementerie is woven in traditional color palettes in order to suit more conservative tastes in interior design. For this reason, designs are often woven to coordinate with the overall color scheme of a room, or the overall color scheme of a fabric that the passementerie is being applied to.

However, passementerie can be used as a striking and dramatic contrast within an interior design scheme—designs do not have to blend into the background! A lot of the designs I use within my own work are based on classical designs from the eighteenth century, given a fabulous update through application, scale, material, and, most importantly—color!

When planning a colorway for your own passementerie designs, start by asking yourself what function you want the design to have—not function in a practical, utilitarian sense, but function in an emotive sense. So, for example: Do I want to conjure a playful effect? Do I want to create a cohesive and harmonious mood? Do I want the passementerie to make a statement?

Listing keywords can be a helpful way to begin to understand what mood you wish to create with color.

The second question to ask is: What are you going to be using your handwoven passementerie for? Is it going to adorn a large cushion or a small lampshade? This is important in terms of how you use color. Generally speaking, a larger item, such as a big cushion, can carry off a bold and complex colorway, whereas a passementerie design for a small lampshade may require a color palette that is a little more pared back. However, there are no rules! Explore and experiment in order to find your own way of designing and using passementerie.

To create my artworks I initially work with color in an intuitive and spontaneous way. I keep sketchbooks filled with different color combinations that I use to inspire my artworks. I collect color in these sketchbooks through yarn samples, drawing, painting, photography, magazine pages, and exhibition postcards. If you love working with color but are not sure where to begin, collecting color swatches of fabric and yarn clippings or paint color chips or simply using a coloring pencil to color lines can be a great place to start.

Color matching to fabric

It is possible to create a passementerie design in a colorway that perfectly complements the fabric to which it is destined to be applied—or pick out a particular color from a fabric design and enhance this through the passementerie. There are many ways to develop a harmonious color palette.

GETTING STARTED

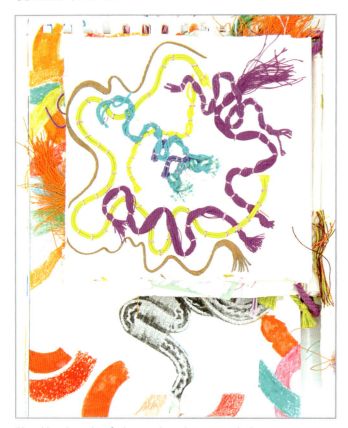 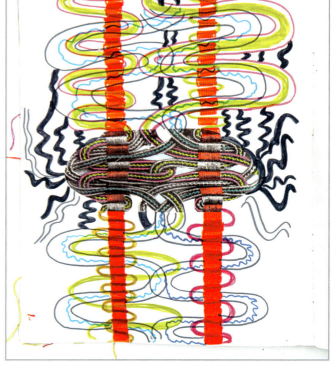

Sketchbook works of plans, color schemes, and ideas.

Color selection tool and software

Take a photo of your fabric and use a free online color selection tool to extract the colors. Then use this color palette to design your trim through drawing, painting, or exploring and sampling with color directly on the loom.

By eye

When planning a colorway for a passementerie design, it can be a very helpful strategy to live with the fabric or object the trimming is going to be applied to, before committing to a final design. Seeing a fabric subconsciously can be a very helpful way to understand what you like about a particular design, and which colors stand out to you at both a close-up and distant view.

SCALLOPS AND PICOTS

A signature element of woven passementerie, the decorative loops that appear on either side of the warp, the selvages, are created using the decorative weft.

Within passementerie, a large loop is called a "scallop" and a small loop is called a "picot."

There is no predetermined size for how big a scallop needs to be or how small a picot should be. If scallop and picot exist within the same design, the larger of the two loops is always a scallop, and the smaller loop is always a picot. A picot can extend wider from the selvage than a scallop, but it is still a picot because it is smaller in height than a scallop.

Pictured below is a simple passementerie design being woven on the loom. Note the two different sizes of loop—a scallop and a picot.
1. Picot.
2. Scallop.

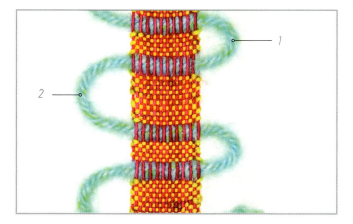

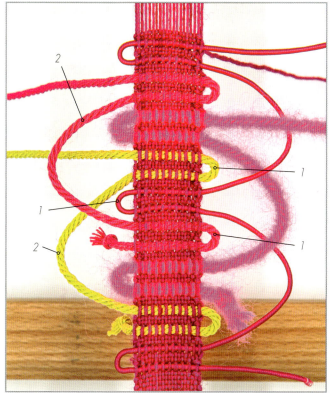

This photo shows the Joséphine Crête on page 123 being woven. Scallops and picots can be as simple or complicated as you like.
1. Picot
2. Scallop

CHOOSING DECORATIVE WEFT MATERIALS

CHOOSING DECORATIVE WEFT MATERIALS

The decorative wefts (DW)—sometimes also known as "supplementary" wefts—are the materials used within passementerie weaving to create the signature scallops and picots in a design. The majority of woven passementerie designs feature decorative wefts, and the more complicated designs—such as the Joséphine Crête on page 123—often use many different decorative wefts within one design to create a rich and intricate pattern.

One of the things I love the most about passementerie is how the designs can be customized to your exact taste through the materials chosen to weave a design. There are so many exciting and varied materials to choose from when selecting DW. High-quality and unusual materials can be difficult to source, but it is worth the effort to seek out specialist suppliers and high-quality haberdashery stores, as you will find all sorts of interesting and unusual materials.

Vintage and antique materials also work beautifully as DW. I have been lucky enough to source vintage wired gimps and rolls of vintage cords from textile fairs and secondhand markets. These materials are so special because they are often a one-off find, which creates a uniqueness to your designs. If you make other crafts, you may find that you have plenty of materials at home to incorporate within your passementerie designs, rather than having to buy new.

Traditional gimp yarn is a very special and luxurious passementerie material that has been used to weave designs for centuries. It is made from a metal wire core that has been tightly covered with yarn, often silk, viscose, or cotton. Due to the metal core, gimp holds its shape beautifully, so it is an ideal material to use to create scallops and picots.

Gimp is still used extensively both in handwoven and commercially produced passementerie. Most weavers have gimp made to their specific requirements and supplied in large quantities. Gimp is very hard to find in smaller lengths, and there are very few stockists of this material. Please see the list on page 159 to discover where you can purchase gimp yarn.

GETTING STARTED

Types of material for decorative wefts

One of the wonderful things about my approach to passementerie is that I believe anything goes when it comes to selecting materials to weave with. I encourage you to experiment with a wide range of materials through on-loom sampling to see what works for you.

However, when beginning to weave passementerie, it is best to select DW that are easy to work with. Once you get used to how passementerie is woven, then you can experiment with a much wider palette of materials.

To begin exploring, I suggest you find a range of smooth and strong tubular cords made from cotton in a range of colors. A cord diameter of around 4–10 mm is an ideal starting point for a beginner. In order to create scallops and picots that hold their shape well once woven and applied to an item, choose a firm material. If you choose a floppy DW material, then the scallops and picots will not hold their shape within a finished design.

Decorative wefts used in the projects

You do not need to use the same DW that I have used within the projects in this book. Using alternative materials will give your trim a different look from the way the designs are pictured. Feel free to experiment with your material selection.

Weaving with decorative wefts

All the projects in this book have been woven using a minimum of two weft yarns—the main body weft (MBW) and the decorative weft.

The MBW is the yarn used for the plain weave sections in each of the projects.

The DW is the material that creates the decorative scallops and picots on either side of the warp selvages. The DW is always woven into its own shed.

See page 55 for helpful tips once you begin weaving.

When weaving with long lengths of DW, it can be very easy to get into a tangle. Using netting shuttles, snap-thread bobbins, or knitting shuttles to hold the decorative weft while weaving all are good methods to employ to keep the DW under control.

1. Traditional wired gimp yarn.
2. Cotton piping cord.
3. Ombre wired ribbon.
4. Metallic braid.
5. Double-faced velvet ribbon.
6. Climbing cord.
7. Paper knitted tube cord.
8. Silver Mylar cord.
9. Flat suede thonging.
10. Paper raffia yarn.

CARING FOR PASSEMENTERIE

Passementerie is designed to be seen, celebrated, and enjoyed! Handweaving passementerie requires an investment of time, passion, and care, and I hope you will keep and enjoy your handcrafted designs for a very long time.

When you remove long lengths of passementerie from the loom, it is best to roll the length around a tube, such as an empty plastic bottle or a piece of cardboard packing roll. This will prevent your passementerie from becoming permanently creased and damaged. Try not to fold your passementerie lengths, as this will distort and damage the design.

Passementerie is often surprisingly robust—depending on the strength of the materials chosen to weave the design. However, the more intricate and heavily looped a design is, the greater the risk of catching and pulling a loop out of place.

As with all textiles, I would advise you to keep your passementerie out of direct sunlight, as this will fade the textile's colors over time. Giving passementerie a quick dusting every now and again will also help keep items clean.

Washing passementerie

Selected designs in this book are attached to objects by using snap fasteners (e.g., scarf trim and bouclé fringe jacket cuffs). This ensures easy removal for cleaning. If you need to clean removable passementerie designs:

1. Fill a sink with warm, clean water with a little wool detergent added. Gently submerge the passementerie until thoroughly soaked.
2. Lightly stir the water bath, making sure that the passementerie remains crease-free. Soak for 10 minutes.
3. Drain the sink and fill with clean, warm water. Gently rinse the passementerie until no soap remains.
4. Lay the passementerie flat on a towel, fold over a section of the towel, and lightly press to remove some of the water.
5. Unfold the towel and leave the design to dry fully.
6. Once dry, iron or gently steam the design (see below for instructions).

Cleaning passementerie that is stitched to an item
Soak a soft cloth in warm water with a little wool detergent added, and gently dab at any marks until they loosen.

Dry-cleaning passementerie
If you would like to dry-clean passementerie, seek out a trusted dry cleaner. When weaving a project, keep a record (including yarn and material samples) of the materials used in the project, in order for the dry cleaner to assess the suitability of materials for cleaning.

Ironing passementerie
After it is removed from the loom or has been washed, the design may benefit from a gentle iron or gentle steam.

To iron
1. Lay the passementerie right side down, wrong side facing up.
2. Place a clean tea towel on top of the design.
3. Using a medium iron setting, very gently press down with the iron, sweeping it along the length of the design.

To steam
1. Lay the passementerie right side down, wrong side facing up.
2. Place a clean tea towel on top of the design.
3. Using a medium iron setting, hold the iron just above the passementerie, without letting the iron touch the tea towel.
4. Gently steam the passementerie length.

GETTING STARTED

WEAVING PASSEMENTERIE ON A FRAME LOOM

Using a frame loom is a great way to create smaller designs and samples. All the designs featured in this book can be woven using a frame loom. The disadvantage of using one is that long lengths cannot be woven because of the way that frame looms work. If you wish to weave long lengths of passementerie, use a different loom, such as a rigid heddle loom.

Materials and equipment

- Frame loom. The one pictured here is the Rico large frame loom 12 × 15.5 in. (30 × 39.5 cm). This loom has four notches to a 1 in. space.
- Two weaving shuttles.
- Metal dining fork.
- Wool needle.
- 2 balls of smooth 100 percent wool DK yarn, ideally in contrasting colors (25 g balls are more than enough). This will be used for the warp, and one color will be used for the main body weft.
- Scissors.
- Sticky tape.
- Tape measure.
- 1 20 in. (50 cm) length of cord to use as the decorative weft. Any material can be used as long as it holds its shape well when curved. This is going to make the scallops and picots on the selvages of the warp.

How to warp a frame loom

The following instructions are suitable for warping a frame loom with four notches to an inch. If your loom has a different number, you will need to warp it according to the notch quantity. These instructions are for double-warping your loom:

First layer of warp

1. Take one DK yarn and slot the tail end into a central notch at the bottom of the frame. Secure in place with a double knot.
2. Guide the yarn to the corresponding notch at the top of the frame, ensuring the yarn is pulled taut, but not so tight that it becomes hard and rigid. (1)
3. At the top of the frame, bring the yarn into the notch to the right of where your first warp yarn is sitting. Guide the yarn

into the corresponding notch at the bottom of the loom, making sure that the yarn is pulled tight as in step 2.

4. **Repeat steps 2–3** until you have four warp yarns (ends) on your loom. You will stop at the bottom of the loom.
5. Cut the yarn, leaving a 10 in. (25 cm) tail. With the warp end slotted into a notch at the bottom, wrap around the bottom of the frame loom under tension. Still keeping the tension, tie the tail end around the last (fourth) warp yarn. Double-knot to secure. Trim back ends. (2)
6. **Double-warp your loom.** Using your second color of DK yarn, repeat steps 1–5 as above, to create a second layer of warp that sits into the same notches as the first warp layer. (3, 4)

Weave the ground ends

7. These are two initial rows of weaving that create a solid foundation for the passementerie weaving to build upon.
8. Using your MBW yarn, cut a length that is three times the width of your frame loom. Tie this length in a double knot around the left-hand side of the frame loom. (5)
9. Using your fingers, lift up the four warp ends in one of the colors (shown here in pink). Slide one of the shuttle sticks flat under these warp ends. Rotate the shuttle so it sits on its side—this action will lift up four warp ends and create an opening in the weaving. Used in this way, the shuttle stick becomes the shed stick, and the opening created in the warp is called the shed. (6)
10. Pass the tied-on ground end yarn through this open shed from left to right. Wrap the yarn around the right-hand side of the loom twice, ensuring that the yarn is pulled taut. Double-knot the yarn around the right-hand side of the loom. (7)
11. Remove the shed stick from the warp. Using your fingers, lift up the other four warp ends in your second color (pictured here in blue) to the right-hand side of the first color of warp ends. (8)

34 |

WEAVING PASSEMENTERIE ON A FRAME LOOM

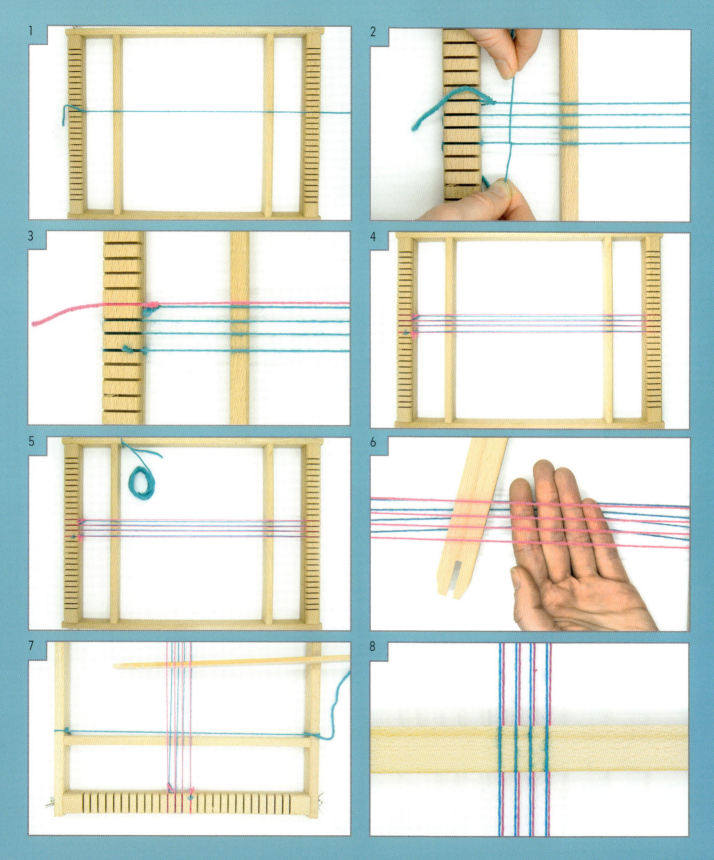

35

GETTING STARTED

12. Weave the ground end through the shed from right to left. Wrap the tail around the left-hand side of the frame loom and double-knot. Trim off any tails. Using your fork, beat down both ground ends so the rows are touching each other. Make sure these rows are straight and are sitting parallel to the bottom of the frame loom. (9, 10)

13. Wind shuttle—see page 45 for instructions.

14. I am using two lengths of 100 percent DK wool yarn in blue as the MBW. I cut two separate lengths of yarn to use together as one, in order to create a thicker result.

Weaving the design

15. This design uses a technique called "plain weave." To create plain weave, lift the two warp colors alternately, using the shed stick. This is the same process used to weave through the ground ends.

16. Lift up the alternate warp yarns (pictured in pink) to the previous row woven (last ground end row). Use the shed stick as before to open the shed. Guide the MBW shuttle through the shed from left to right, leaving an 8 in. (20 cm) tail of yarn on the left side of the warp. This weft tail will remain here for the duration of the weaving. (11)

17. Use the fork to beat the row of weaving down, making sure the row is sitting straight and horizontally even. Remove the shed stick.

18. Change the shed to lift up the alternate warp end colors. Weave MBW from right to left through the warp. Beat down and remove the shed stick. Repeat until four rows in total have been woven. (12)

19. Change the shed. Weave your decorative weft length (pictured here in orange) through the shed from left to right, leaving a 1 in. (2.5 cm) tail on the left-hand side of the warp. (13)

20. Change shed. Weave 11 rows with MBW, making sure to change the shed for each row of weaving. After row 11, change the shed and weave the DW through the warp from right to left, creating a 1 in. (2.5 cm) wide scallop on the right-hand side of the selvage. Beat down well. (14)

21. Change shed. Weave seven rows with MBW, making sure to change the shed for each row of weaving. After row 7, change the shed and weave the DW through the warp from left to right, creating a ¾ in. (1.9 cm) wide picot on the left-hand side of the selvage. Beat down well. (15)

22. Continue weaving the design as above until it reaches your desired length. Weave four rows of plain weave with MBW to finish your design. Try not to weave any closer than 3 in. (7 cm) from the top of your frame loom—any closer than this and the weaving becomes very tight and extremely difficult to weave. (16)

Removing from the loom and weaving in weft tails

Follow the instructions on page 57 to learn how to remove the weaving from the loom, and those on page 58 to learn how to weave in the weft tails.

WEAVING PASSEMENTERIE ON A FRAME LOOM

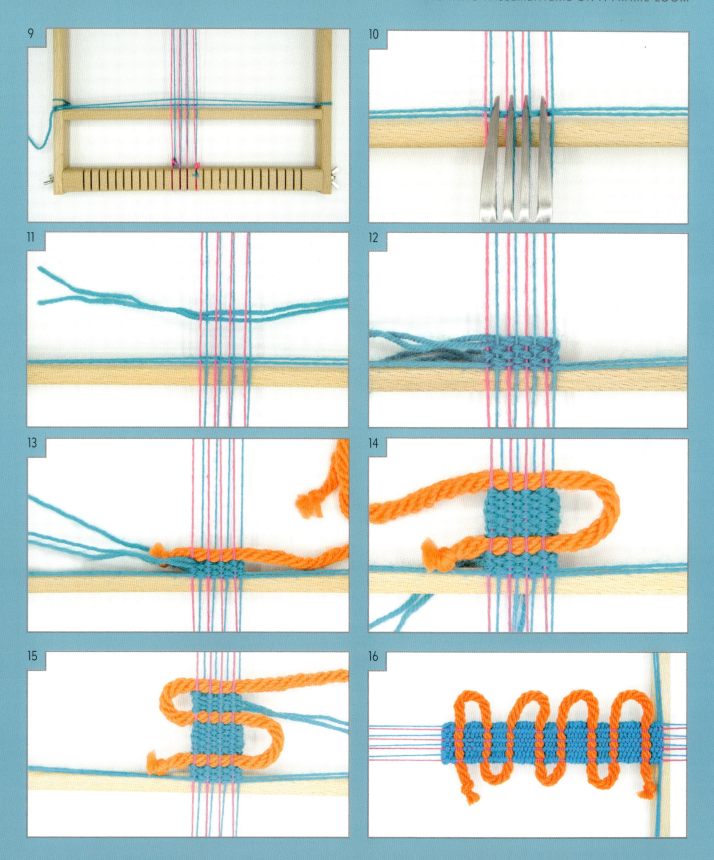

37

GETTING STARTED

WARPING A RIGID HEDDLE LOOM

Calculating warp length

For each project in this book, you will see that a suggested warp measurement is listed for a particular design. This suggested warp measurement has been worked out on the basis of the following calculation:

Length of finished project
+ take-up (10 percent of desired woven length)
+ extra yarn waste and mistakes
= suggested measurement

Take-up is the natural warp shrinkage that occurs when the finished length is removed from the tension of the loom. To counter this, I like to add a good bit extra to the length of my warps, just in case something goes wrong along the way!

Let's say we are going to weave a finished passementerie length of 60 in. (152 cm):

60 in. (length of design required)
+ 6 in. / 15 cm (take-up)
+ 20 in. / 51 cm (for waste and mistakes)
= total warp length of 86 in. (218 cm)
So, you need 2.3 yd. (2.1 m) to weave your design.

Materials and equipment

· G-clamps.
· One long table, or two smaller tables.
· Reed.
· Rigid heddle loom.
· Sheets of clean, white letter/printing paper.
· Threading hook.
· Total warp length required—see above for instructions showing how to calculate warp length.
· Warp yarn.
· Warping post.

Method

These are the instructions for warping using the direct method on your rigid heddle.

If you know how to warp a rigid heddle loom, the process for warping for passementerie is almost the same, with a few small changes. The main difference is the narrower width of the warp for passementerie weaving. When winding the passementerie warp onto the loom, care must be taken to ensure that the entire warp is being wound on under very high tension, taking particular care that the edges do not loosen off tension while being wound around the beam.

The other difference is the use of warp paper, rather than the cardboard warping sticks that are often supplied with a rigid heddle loom. For warp paper, you can use regular white letter paper. The warp paper is inserted between the layers of warp while the warp is being wound around the back beam / roller of the loom. The paper creates a barrier and stops the layers of warp from rubbing on each other, which can cause warp breakages, among other problems.

1. The length of warp required to weave a project determines the length needed between the back of the loom and the warping post. For example, if your project requires a total warp length of 2.3 yd. / 2.1m, a space of 2.3 yd. is required between the back of the loom and the warping post. Use a long table, or two separated tables. Clamp the warping post securely to the table. At the other end of the table, clamp the loom securely to the table, ensuring the back of the loom faces the warping post. (1)

2. The back of the loom has a cutout section directly below the cog. Ensure the back cog and front cog brakes are engaged. (2)

3. Insert the reed into the front reed rest position.

4. At the back of the loom, tie the warp yarn securely around the back warp beam stick, slightly to the left-hand side of the center of the reed. Sit the ball of yarn on the floor in a bowl, directly below the back of the loom. (3)

WARPING A RIGID HEDDLE LOOM

5. Identify a slot in the reed that is slightly to the left-hand side of the center of the reed. Pass the threading hook through this slot from front to back. The hook should be facing the back of the loom. Catch the warp yarn on the hook to create a loop. **(4)**

6. Pull this loop through the slot in the reed. Continue to pull on this loop until it reaches the warping post. **(5, 6)**

| 39

GETTING STARTED

6

7

7. Loop the yarn over the post. (6)

Very important tip: Ensure that the warp is kept under tension throughout the warping process. A good warp tension will feel springy when pushed down.

8. At the back of the loom, take the ball of yarn and wrap this over the top and underneath the back beam stick. (7, 8)
9. Pass the threading hook through the next slot in the reed to the right-hand side of the slot just used (as you look at the reed from the back of the loom).
10. Repeat steps 6–8 until the desired quantity of warp yarns (also called ends) have been put on the loom. In this case I have dressed the loom with eight warp ends. (9)
11. When the desired quantity of warp ends has been reached, cut it from the ball at the back warp beam stick, leaving a tail roughly 12 in. (30 cm) long. Under tension, wrap the cut warp yarn twice around the back warp beam stick. Knot securely. (10, 11)
12. Ask a friend to stand behind the warping post. Lift the loops from the post, keeping a firm tension on the warp. Stand behind the loom and begin to roll the warp around the back warp beam, using the back cog. Keep an even, firm tension on the warp throughout the entire winding process. (12)

WARPING A RIGID HEDDLE LOOM

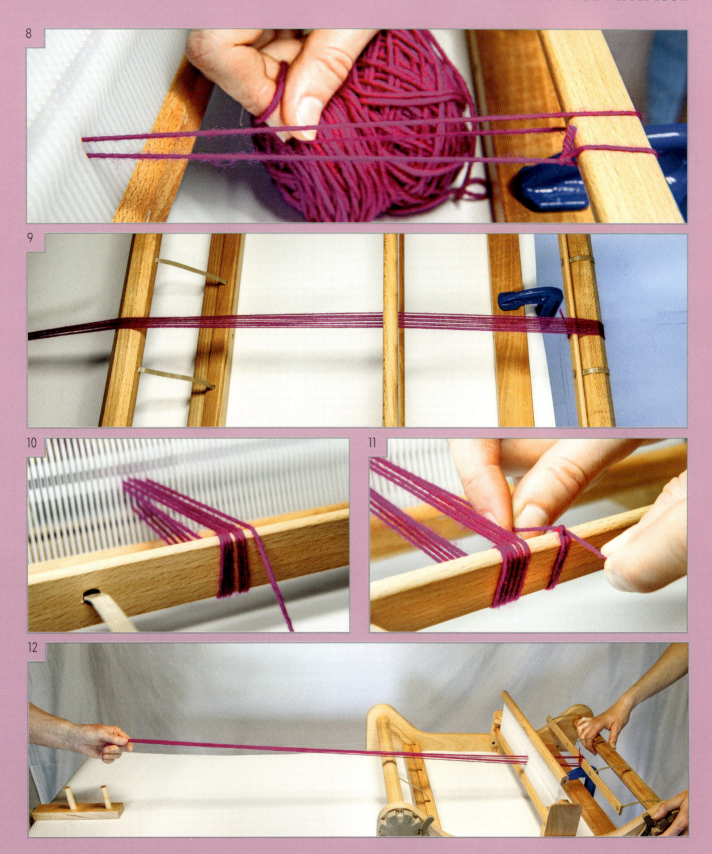

41

GETTING STARTED

13. Wind the warp around the back beam until the wound layer of warp touches the top layer of warp. Stop winding. (12a, 12b)
14. Place a landscape sheet of letter paper underneath the warp where it is touching the wound layer of warp. (13, 13a)
15. Continue winding on the warp as above, making sure that a fresh piece of paper is placed between the layers of warp when the previous sheet is almost wound around the beam. Stop winding the warp when there is approximately 15 in. (38 cm) of unwound warp in front of the reed.

Threading the loom

1. At the front of the loom and starting on the left-hand side of the warp, take the first warp end. Using the threading hook, pass this warp end through the eye to the right-hand side of the slot. The yarn in the slot stays in the slot. (14, 15)
2. Continue working across the reed, moving every alternate warp end into an eye with the threading hook. Half the warp ends will be threaded through an eye, and the remaining half of the warp ends will be threaded through a slot. (16)

Tying the warp onto the front beam / roller stick

1. Once the warp has been sleyed in the reed, it needs to be tied onto the front beam / roller stick before the weaving can begin.
2. Divide the warp bunch (eight ends) into two bunches (four ends each). Take the first bunch over and around the back of the front warp beam / roller stick. Bring the tails up. Pull firmly on the bunch and tie the tails around the bunch in a *single* knot. (17)
3. Repeat step 2 with the second bunch of yarn. Check the tension in the first bunch and adjust by pulling on the yarn tails if needed. Once the tension is correct, tie a second knot. Repeat with the second bunch, making sure that the tension on the yarn is identical to the first bunch. You are now ready to weave.

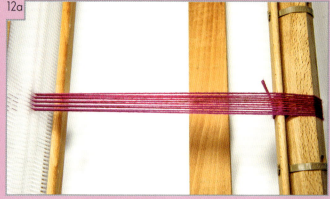

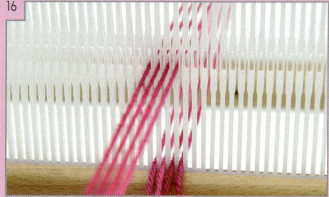

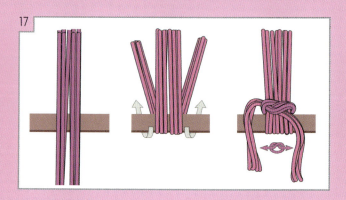

WARPING A RIGID HEDDLE LOOM

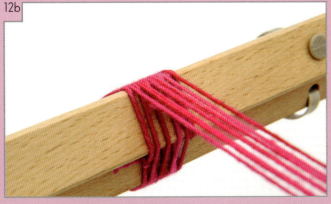

12b

13a

15

Warp tension

The tension of your warp during weaving will greatly affect the quality of your weaving. Creating an even tension through the warp, and maintaining this tension throughout the entirety of the weaving, is critical to ensure that your project is a success. Don't worry if you are not an experienced weaver—learning how to correctly tension your warp comes from trial and error. Start off a project with tension that is even; too loose or too tight can make the weaving much harder than it needs to be.

Tension tips

For passementerie weaving, the warp tension needs to be firm, but not tight, in order to support the many interchanges between warp and wefts.

Weaving passementerie on a loosely tensioned warp will be extremely difficult, and you will not be able to achieve a good result. Conversely, weaving on an extremely tight warp will be extremely difficult too—it distorts the design, and a tight warp hurts your hands, plus the warp is liable to break.

The advantage of using a rigid heddle loom is the ability to alter the warp tension through tightening or loosening the cog attached to the back roller / beam. A good way of knowing whether your warp is correctly tensioned is to check the "springiness" of the warp with your hand. Once the warp is tied onto your front beam stick, place your palm across the warp and push down. The warp should spring, a bit like jumping on a trampoline. This is a good warp tension. As the weaving progresses, maintain this tension. You may well find that the tension needs adjusting at various points within the weaving.

It is so much easier to make sure your warp tension is correct right at the beginning of a project.

How to fix tension issues

Tension issues can occur at any stage of a project, and sometimes it is hard to work out why this has happened!

- Often, weavers experience tension issues because the warp yarn they have chosen is not suitable to be used as a warp. Knowing which yarns work, and which yarns don't, comes from experience.
- If you suddenly lose tension, check to make sure that the pawls that hold the front and back warp rollers/beams are in still in place.
- If you notice that tension is too loose over small sections or a length of selvage, wedge a small piece of cardboard underneath the warp, directly on top of the back roller/beam. This will add a little extra height underneath the loose warp threads to take up some of the slack.

| 43

GETTING STARTED

WINDING SHUTTLES AND BOBBINS

Weaving shuttles come in various sizes and designs. Both a small stick shuttle and a small boat shuttle are very useful for weaving passementerie. A small boat shuttle is ideal if you are weaving a long, continuous length of a design. The choice of what shuttle to use largely depends on an individual weaver's preference. Stay away from long stick shuttles and long boat shuttles, as these can be unwieldy to manage due to the narrow width of passementerie warps.

How to wind a bobbin for a boat shuttle

1. Pictured here from left to right: a cardboard bobbin/quill, and 8 in. (20 cm) long boat shuttle. (1)
2. Pinch the end of the yarn against the bobbin with your thumb. Wind the yarn around the bobbin under slight tension. Wind from the middle to the top. Then wind top to bottom. Keep winding bottom to top until the bobbin is full of yarn and the yarn is distributed evenly. (2)
3. Do not overwrap the bobbin, as an overfilled bobbin will get stuck in the yarn shuttle. Cut off from the ball of yarn. (3)

How to wind a small stick shuttle

4. Unwind a length of yarn from the ball. Hold the stick shuttle in one hand. Pick up the yarn and pinch 2 in. (5 cm) from the end of the yarn. Hold this pinched area against the shuttle stick while the yarn is wrapped under slight tension around the shuttle, from top to bottom. (4, 5)
5. Continue wrapping the yarn around the shuttle until there are 10 wraps of yarn complete. Don't overfill the shuttle with yarn, as this can cause it to get caught within the weaving. Cut off from the ball of yarn when complete. (6)

PLYING MAIN BODY WEFT YARN

Weaving with plied yarns is a great way of introducing a range of textures, colors, and materials into your passementerie weaving through the main body weft yarn (MBW). Plying yarns is also a great way of making a thin yarn (such as a lace-weight mohair yarn) thicker, so it is more suitable to use as the MBW.

The Wisteria border for a scarf on page 135 is woven using four different colors and textures of yarn plied together to create a fun, contemporary tweed effect.

The Dahlia braid on page 107 is woven using lace-weight mohair yarn. Seven strands of mohair have been plied together and used as the MBW, creating a thicker bunch of yarn.

In this design, I have plied four different-colored yarns together to create one thicker, multidimensional MBW. (7)

1. Select four weft yarns—they can be different colors, textures, or thicknesses.
2. Take a strand of each yarn and hold them together in your hand as one bunch.
3. Wind this bunch around a yarn bobbin or yarn shuttle under a little tension, ensuring that each yarn winds around the bobbin/shuttle neatly.

7

| 45

GETTING STARTED

PLAIN WEAVE

All the projects in this book are woven using a technique called "plain weave" (also known as tabby). This is a technique that is used in the majority of passementerie weaving, whether on a large-scale commercial basis or created by an individual weaver.

What is plain weave?

Weaving is described as a constructed textile. A constructed textile is made by processes that involve connecting yarns together through interlacing, such as weaving. Within weaving, the design that is formed by this interlacing is called a structure rather than a pattern.

Plain weave is a woven structure, and of all woven structures it is the simplest to weave. Plain weave works by interlacing the warp yarn with the weft yarn in a one-under, one-over construction. Plain weave has two benefits for passementerie weaving—the structure creates a firm and stable textile, and plain weave does not create a complicated design on the surface of the weaving. **(1)**

Using the plain-weave structure to make passementerie ensures that both warp and weft yarns are held in place firmly. Since plain weave does not create a decorative design on the surface of the weaving, all the attention is given to the decorative scallops and picots that form the highly decorative selvages. **(2)**

How to plain weave on a rigid heddle loom

Plain weave is woven by alternately raising and then lowering set warp ends with the reed—doing this on a rigid heddle loom is extremely easy. Once the warp is tied on securely to the front beam stick, the weaving can commence. On a rigid heddle loom there are three different positions that the reed can sit within: the rest, up-weaving, and down-weaving positions.

1. **Rest position**—where the reed sits in a neutral position when no weaving is happening. **(3)**
2. **Up-weaving position**—by raising the reed to this position, half the warp ends are raised, while half the warp threads remain flat. **(4)**
3. An opening is created by this separation of the warp ends— this is called the shed. **(5)**
4. The weft yarn, wrapped around a shuttle or a bobbin, is passed through the open shed, leaving a tail on the left-hand side of the warp approx 6 in. (15 cm) long. This weft tail is later woven into the design; see page 58 for step-by-step instructions. **(6)**

PLAIN WEAVE

1

2
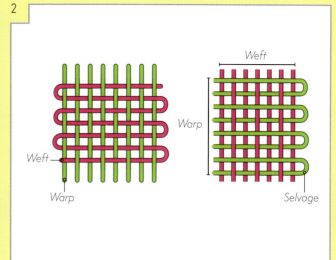

3

4

5

6
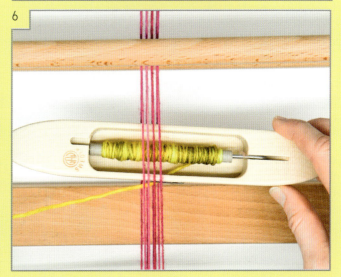

| 47

GETTING STARTED

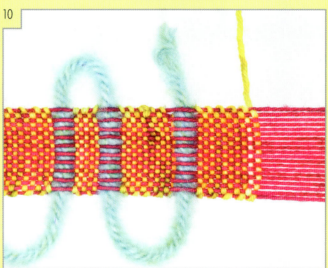

PLAIN WEAVE

5. After the weft yarn has passed through the shed, the reed is removed from the rest position and brought forward to firmly push the first row of weaving down—this is called beating. **(7)**

6. **Down-weaving position**—by lowering the reed to this position, warp ends are lowered. **(8)**

7. The now-lowered warp ends are the same ones that remained flat in step 2. The warp ends that were raised up in step 2 now sit flat when the reed is lowered to the down weaving position. The weft yarn is then passed back through this newly opened shed, and the reed is bought down again to beat down the rows of weaving. **(9)**

8. In order to continue to weave plain weave, the shed must be changed after every row of weaving. To change the shed, the reed needs to alternate between being raised into the up position and then being lowered into the down position, with the weft yarn being passed through the shed each time. This raising-and-lowering process alternates the warp ends that are in use in order to create a balanced woven textile—a plain weave. When a section of plain weave has been woven, look closely at the surface of the weaving. If you have used a weft yarn that is roughly equal in diameter to the warp yarn, you will see a balanced surface—both warp yarns and weft yarns will be visible.

9. If you have used a weft yarn that is similar in diameter to the warp yarn, both the weft yarn and the warp yarn will be equally visible, as pictured here. **(10)**

10. Using a weft yarn that is thicker than the warp yarn results in all the warp being covered. Only the weft (*pictured in yellow*) will be visible. **(11)**

GETTING STARTED

WEAVING THROUGH THE GROUND ENDS

After the warp has been tied on to the front beam stick, three rows of foundation weaving (the ground ends) are needed. These ground ends create a stable foundation base for the passementerie weaving.

Select a smooth and strong yarn to use for the ground ends; garden string or kitchen twine is ideal. The ground ends are woven through the warp under some tension. They are wrapped and knotted around either side of the front beam stick. This not only creates a stable foundation for the passementerie weaving, but the ground ends also balance out the warp tension as well as ensuring that the selvages of the warp are sitting flat and even.

Method
1. Cut one length of strong yarn approximately three times the width of your loom. Wrap the yarn tail around the left-hand side of the front beam stick. Tie securely.
2. Open the shed. Weave through the tied-on ground end from left to right. Pull the ground end so it is taut. Wrap the tail under tension around the right-hand side of the front beam stick. Knot securely. (1)
3. Change the shed. Weave the ground end through the warp from right to left under tension. Wrap the tail under tension around the left-hand side of the front beam stick. Knot securely. (2, 3)
4. Repeat step 2. Once knotted on the right-hand side of the front beam stick, cut off the remaining ground end tail. (4, 5)

Once the ground ends are woven through the warp as above, the passementerie weaving can begin.

WEAVING THROUGH GROUND ENDS

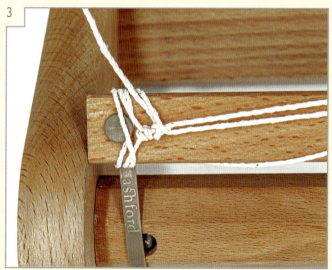

| 51

GETTING STARTED

HOW TO USE GUIDE STRINGS

The use of guide strings is a straightforward way of ensuring that scallops and picots are a consistent size while weaving a length of passementerie. In this example, I have demonstrated how to use a pair of guide strings to create scallops. Any quantity of guide strings can be used simultaneously while you are weaving—simply increase the quantity to suit the complexity of your design.

Materials and equipment

- Long lengths* of strong, nonelastic yarn. Garden string/twine is ideal.
- Multiple weights.* 3 in. (7.6 cm) metal G-clamps are ideal. Specific loom weights can be purchased if preferred.

*Each individual guide string needs its own weight.

Method

1. Guide strings are added to your loom once your warp is ready for weaving. Weave about ½ in. (1.3 cm) using main body weft to begin your design. Determine the width of your desired scallops. In this example I am creating scallops ¾ in. (2 cm) wide.
2. Cut your guide string yarn so it measures 15 percent longer than the length of trimming that you are going to be weaving. Thread the guide string (shown in light-pink string) through a slot in the reed, ¾ in. (2 cm) away from the left-hand side of the warp. Tie this guide string securely around the front beam stick. The long length of guide string is now facing the back of the loom. (1)
3. Repeat step 2 to the right-hand side of the warp, using the second guide string length. (2)
4. At the back of the loom, tie each individual guide string length to a separate weight. Ensure that the weight hangs freely from the back of the loom, about 12 in. (30 cm) below the back warp beam. Ensure that you can undo the knot in the future to release more guide string length as required. (3)
5. Continue weaving your design as normal. When ready to create your first scallop, pass the decorative weft over the top and underneath one guide string, making sure not to pull on the guide string. Weave the decorative weft through the warp as normal. Repeat step 5 as many times as required. Make sure not to inadvertently pull on the guide string—this must remain straight and vertical throughout the duration of the weaving. As the design builds up, the guide strings will be rolled around the front warp beam alongside the weaving. When you need more guide string length, undo the knotted weight, retie to extend the length, and continue weaving. (4)

HOW TO USE GUIDE STRINGS

1
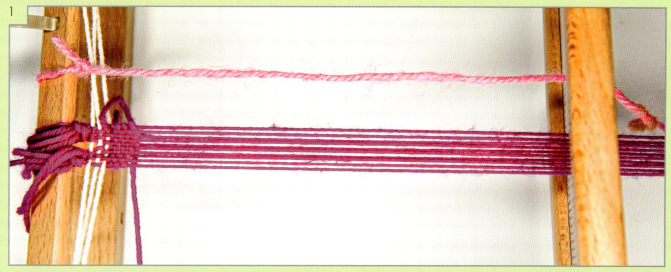

2

3

4

| 53

GETTING STARTED

WEAVING WITH DECORATIVE WEFT

Whether you are using a frame loom or a rigid heddle loom to weave passementerie, you still have to take care with the placement of the MBW row that weaves immediately after a row of DW. This is because the MBW can occasionally skip underneath the edge warp thread when the MBW is woven back through the warp. If this happens it can cause the edge to become a little unstable. However, there are two easy fixes to prevent this. Try both of these methods to see which one you prefer aesthetically—both of them will ensure that the warp is held in place securely. I have used both methods for the projects in this book.

Method
Option 1

1. A row of multicolored DW has been woven through the warp. The next step is to change the shed and weave through the MBW. **(1)**
2. A row of MBW (*pictured in yellow*) woven through the warp from right to left. This row has not yet been beaten into place with the reed. In this example the MBW row has been woven on top of the DW. Weaving the MBW on top of the DW in this way will ensure that the warp edge sitting immediately underneath the DW is held in place securely. **(2)**
3. Shows three rows of MBW woven above the decorative weft. Note the loop of yellow MBW sitting on top of the DW. As the weaving progresses, the MBW will need to be looped on top of the DW only occasionally, where you notice that the edge warp thread will not be caught by the MBW. **(3)**
4. Shows the MBW wrapping over the DW. **(4)**

Option 2

This is a good method to employ if you do not wish the MBW to sit on top of the DW. The MBW is taken underneath the DW as follows:

5. One row of DW has been woven through the warp from left to right. The next step is to change the shed. With the shed open, guide your finger through the shed and gently press down onto the last warp end. Here, I am holding down the last warp end on the right-hand side of the warp, as the MBW needs to be woven through from the right-hand side of the warp to the left-hand side. **(5)**
6. Weave through the MBW, making sure to take the MBW on top of the warp end that was held down in step 1. **(6)**
7. This results in the MBW being taken underneath the DW. Look closely at the right-hand warp end. The MBW is sitting on top of the last warp end, securely holding the end in place. **(7)**
8. This shows a trim on the loom being woven using option 2. Note how the MBW is not sitting on top of the DW. **(8)**

GETTING STARTED

REMOVING WEAVING FROM THE LOOM

1. At the end of the design, make sure to weave a block of plain weave. **(1)**
2. Let off the warp tension from the back beam. Roll the warp forward until there is a long section of unwoven warp in front of the reed. Immediately in front of the reed, cut through two warp ends only. These two warps ends will be knotted together. **(2)**
3. Keep tension on these two warp ends with your fingers. Pinch the yarns halfway down their length with the thumb and finger of your left hand. **(3)**
4. Keep your thumb and finger pinched on the halfway point. With your right hand, pinch the top of the warp yarn under a little tension. Move the top of the warp yarn down so it is roughly level with your other hand. **(4)**
5. Twist the pinched yarn in your left hand toward you in order to create a small loop. **(5)**
6. Feed the yarn tail in your right hand through the loop. **(6)**
7. Pull some of the length through this loop. Using your thumb and finger, slide and tighten the knot toward the top of the plain-weave section. **(7)**
8. The knot needs to be positioned as close to the top of the plain-weave section as possible without distorting the top of the weaving. **(8)**
9. Repeat steps 2–8 until all the warp ends have been knotted in pairs. Cut off the warp ends no closer than ½ in. (1 cm) away from the top of the knot.
10. Once the top warp ends have been removed from the loom, the same overhand-knot process is repeated with the bottom warp ends (which are rolled around the beam at the beginning of the design). However, there is one difference when it comes to finishing these warp ends. Please see the following section.

7

8

GETTING STARTED

WEAVING IN MAIN BODY WEFT TAILS

Once the weaving is removed from the loom, the MBW weft tails are woven into the back of the design, using a wool needle. This weaving-in process creates a secure and invisible finish from the front of the design.

The MBW used to weave this design is blue. I have demonstrated the weaving-in technique by using a pink yarn for clarity's sake.

1. Turn over the trim so the wrong side is facing up. Thread the weft tail (*indicated in pink*) through a wool needle (1)
2. Catch the needle underneath one of the woven "stitches" on the back of the work. Make sure not to catch under one of the selvage stitches. Slide the needle through this stitch and pull through the length of the weft tail firmly but gently in an upward direction. (2)
3. Turn the needle downward. Slide the needle through another stitch and pull through the length of the weft tail. (3)
4. Two "catches" are sufficient if the design is not going to be handled frequently. Repeat steps 2 and 3 once more if the design is going to be moved around more often. (4)
5. Cut off the excess weft tail. (5)
6. Repeat the same weaving-in process until all the weft tails have been woven in.

WEAVING IN MAIN BODY WEFT TAILS

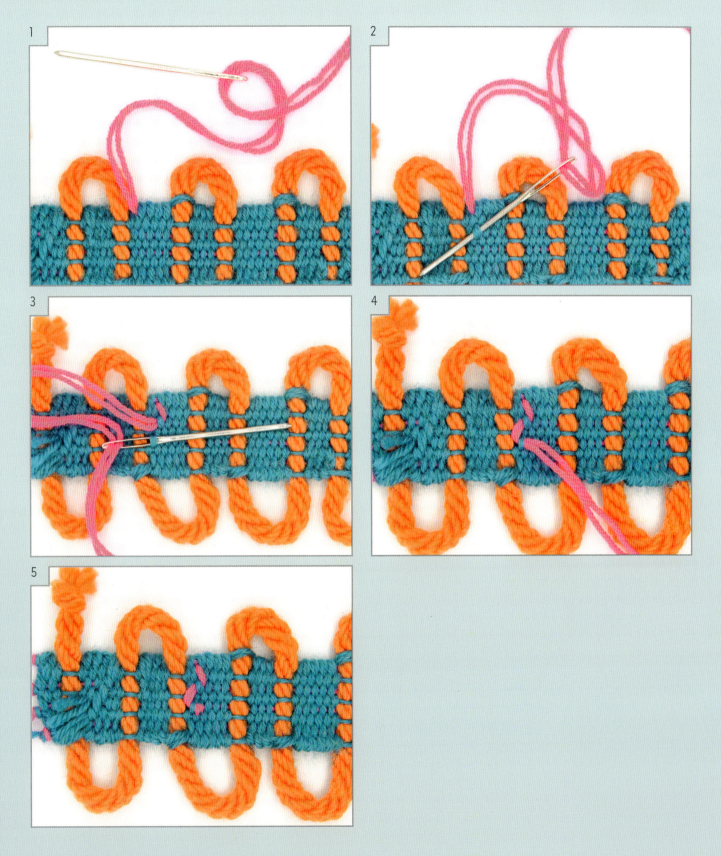

59

TROUBLESHOOTING

FIXING A BROKEN WARP END

Sometimes a warp end can break, for a variety of reasons—the warp tension may be too loose or too tight. Alternatively, faults in the yarn can cause the yarn to snap while weaving. If your warp yarn continually breaks, this strongly suggests that the yarn you have used is not suitable for a warp. See "Selecting warp yarn" guide on page 28.

Snapped warp

1. Pictured here is a warp end that has snapped in two. Pass the snapped warp end that is coming from the back beam out of the reed. (1)
2. Pictured here is the back beam of the loom. Trim the snapped warp end shorter, so there is a length of approximately 3 in. (7.5 cm). (2)
3. Cut a length of the yarn used as the warp, about twice the length of your loom. Tie one end of the new yarn length securely to the broken warp end just in front of the loom back beam. (3)
4. Pass this new length of yarn through the correct slot or eye in the reed. Take the original, shorter length of broken warp yarn and place it so the length is running down the weaving. This length will stay here for the duration of the weaving.
5. Place a pin horizontally through the weaving. Wrap the new length of warp yarn around the pin in a figure eight, making sure that the wrapped length of warp yarn is sitting roughly in the gap created by the original broken warp end. When the pin is full, cut off the remaining new warp tail. (4) Continue weaving your design as normal.
6. When the design is removed from the loom, take out the pin and trim the remaining warp yarn tail off. Trim the shorter warp tail off too.

FIXING A BROKEN WARP END

| 61

TROUBLESHOOTING

WHAT TO DO IF THE DECORATIVE WEFT RUNS OUT

The easiest way of dealing with decorative weft that runs out is to simply weave in a fresh length of DW, leaving long weft tails that are then stitched to the back of the design to create a false scallop or picot.

1. Here the decorative weft has run out of length on the left-hand side of the warp. The next part of the design is to create a scallop on the left-hand selvage. When the decorative weft runs out, make sure to leave a tail of DW approximately 2 in. (5.5 cm) long that dangles from the selvage on the side of the warp that the scallop/picot needs to be created on. This tail will remain here until the design is removed from the loom. **(1)**
2. Take a new length of DW. Weave this through the warp, leaving a tail of approximately 7 in. (13 cm) on the side of the warp where the scallop/picot needs to be created. This tail will remain here until the design is removed from the loom. **(2)**
3. Continue weaving your design as normal, leaving the DW tails in place. Once the design has been removed from the loom, a false scallop/picot is going to be created, using the weft tails, a regular sharps needle, and sewing thread. **(3)**
4. Fold the shorter DW tail onto the reverse side of the trim, making sure to create a neat fold on the selvage **(4)**
5. Couch down the short tail onto the reverse side of the design, using a needle and thread. Close up. **(5)**
6. Trim off the remaining tail once couched. **(6)**
7. The longer DW tail is going to create a false scallop/picot. Fold this length onto the reverse side of the design, creating a false scallop/picot on the selvage. Couch down this length onto the reverse side of the design, checking that the placement of the false scallop/picot matches the woven scallops/picots. **(7)**
8. Close up. **(8)**
   Trim off the remaining tail once couched.
9. Take care over the placement of the false scallop/picot to ensure that it blends in well with the design. Pictured here showing the front of the design, the false scallop join is hardly visible. **(9)**

WHAT TO DO IF THE DECORATIVE WEFT RUNS OUT

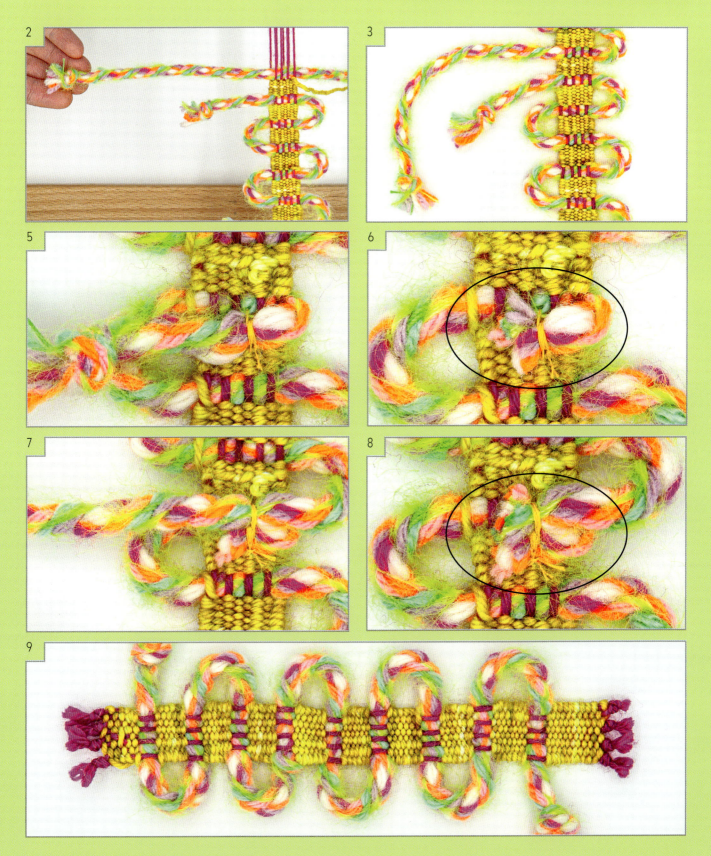

TROUBLESHOOTING

COMMON SELVAGE PROBLEMS

Sometimes it can be challenging to weave straight selvages, especially when weaving designs with multiple interchanges between warp, weft, and decorative weft. Below are some troubleshooting tips for common selvage issues that you may experience:

Overtensioned selvages

1. Here the main body weft yarn (MBW), in yellow, has been pulled too tightly on the selvages when the MBW yarn is weaving through the warp. This causes the selvages to narrow dramatically, which in turn causes the warp to become overly tight and constricted. (1)

Weaving straight edges

2. The MBW (*in yellow*) has been well tensioned on either selvage. This results in straight selvages on either side of the warp. (2)
3. To weave straight selvages, care must be taken when weaving the MBW yarn through the warp. Gently take the MBW yarn through the open shed, but don't pull through the entire MBW yarn length yet, as pictured here. (3)
4. With one hand, pinch the little loop formed by the MBW yarn on the outside of the selvage. With your other hand, hold the MBW yarn length. Gently pull through the MBW yarn length, gradually loosening off the tension on the selvage yarn loop as the MBW is pulled through. (4)

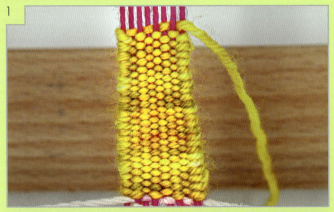

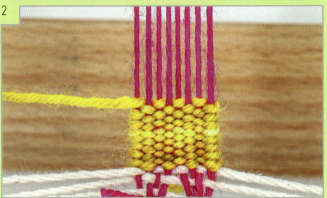

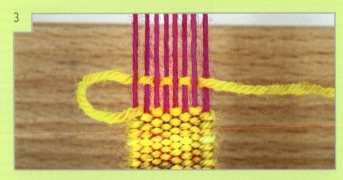

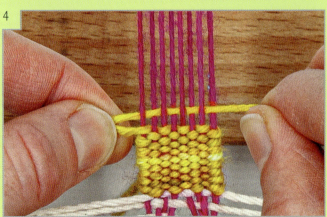

COMMON SELVAGE PROBLEMS

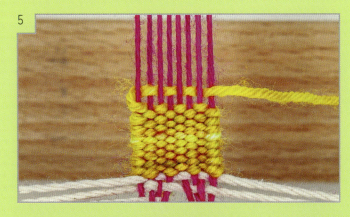

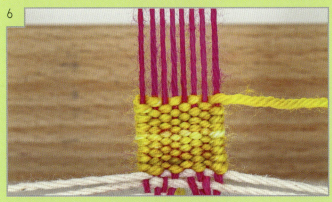

5. Keep gently pulling the MBW yarn length through the warp until the MBW yarn is just wrapping around the edge warp end on the selvage, but without putting any pressure on the edge warp end. **(5)**
6. Beat down the MBW yarn. Check that the MBW yarn is wrapping around the selvage warp end without putting any pressure on this end. **(6)**

Loosely tensioned selvages

7. If the warp selvages are too loosely tensioned, the warp can widen out, which, over time, creates a unstable textile. Pictured here are selvages that are too loosely woven, indicated by larger loops on either selvage. **(7)**
8. To ensure that the selvages are evenly tensioned in the first instance, follow the above steps from the beginning of the weaving. If you notice that edges are too loose during weaving, it is best practice to unpick the rows of weaving back to where the loose selvages began. Reweave the area, making sure to correctly tension the warp selvages.
9. Loose warp selvages can also occur if the entire warp is too loosely tensioned. A well-tensioned warp should have a spring to the warp ends when touched. If the warp is too loose, the warp ends will appear saggy. Another way of telling whether the warp is too loose is to see how the reed is sitting—if the reed keeps falling out of the rest position, it suggests that the warp is too loose. Tighten the warp by using the back beam cog.

OFF-LOOM PASSEMENTERIE SKILLS

TASSEL MAKING USING THE EMBROIDERY SKEIN METHOD

Dangling from cushion corners, or used to add extra embellishments to a handwoven length of passementerie, a cotton tassel is the icing on the cake in the world of passementerie. The variety of tassels is enormous—they can be exquisitely designed and very complicated to create, taking many hours of handcraftsmanship to complete. Or, as in the instructions provided here, they can be made simply and quickly by using an ingenious embroidery skein method. As well as it being incorporated into particular projects in this book, you could use this same method to create tassels to adorn keys, door handles, curtains, or any other object your imagination can think of.

Equipment

To make one 3 in. (7.6 cm) long tassel, you will need:

- 1 skein of 100 percent cotton DMC size 25 special embroidery thread in your color of choice. This skein has 8.7 yd. (8 m) of cotton.
- Sharp embroidery scissors.
- Tape measure.
- Wool/tapestry needle (blunt end).

Method

1. Keep the paper wrappers around the embroidery skein. Pull the end of the skein and cut two lengths of cotton 13 in. (33 cm) long. Fold both cut lengths in half. **(1)**
2. Take one of the folded cut lengths. Tie a loop about 2 in. (5 cm) from the top. Put to one side. **(2)**
3. Take the skein of thread and fold in half to find the halfway point. Put to one side. **(3)**
4. Take the looped and knotted thread length and open the ends. Lay this thread length flat on the table, with the loop pointing upward (this loop will become the tassel hanging cord) and the tails running parallel horizontally. Place the skein on top of the thread length, with the halfway point of the skein sitting directly on top of the knot. **(4)**
5. Take the horizontal thread lengths and tie around the halfway point of the skein. Check that the knot is sitting exactly at the halfway point of the skein before pulling tightly to secure the knot. **(5)**
6. Fold the skein in half. Remove both plastic wrappers from the skein. Take the longer plastic wrapper and slide it down the folded skein from the hanging loop. Stop when the plastic wrapper is sitting approximately ¾ in. (1.9 cm) from the knot holding the hanging loop. **(6)**
7. Take the other 13 in. (33 cm) long length of thread. This will become the tassel head binding cord. Take this length and measure down to just a little longer than the tassel. Put your finger on this point. Fold the rest of the length so a loop is created where your finger is. **(7)**

TASSEL MAKING USING THE EMBROIDERY SKEIN METHOD

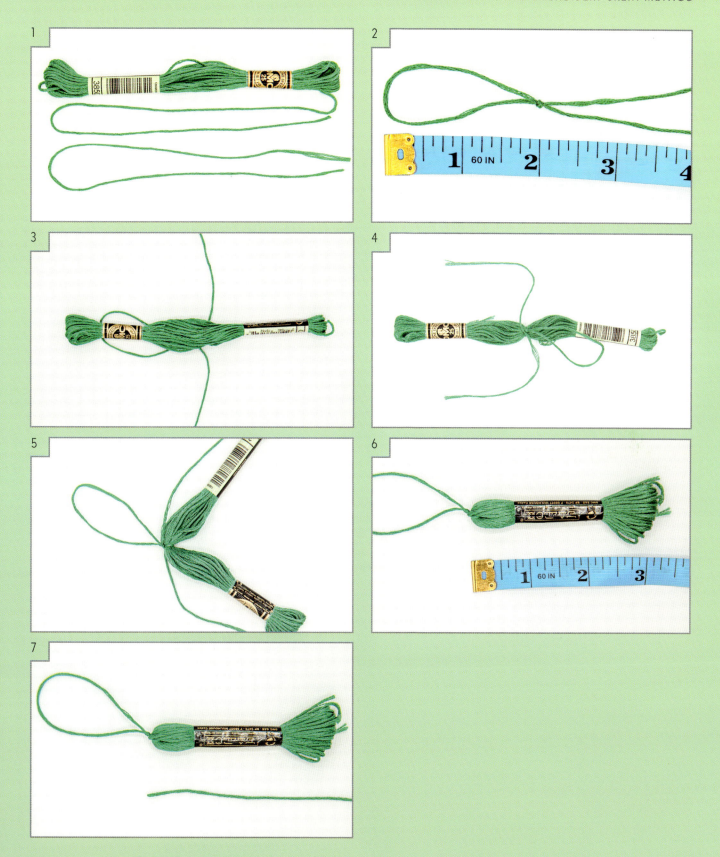

OFF-LOOM PASSEMENTERIE SKILLS

8

9

10

The following steps are demonstrated using an orange thread length instead of the second green, to clearly show the method:

8. Pick up this folded, looped length (shown in orange). Hold the loop in place near the top of the paper wrapper on the tassel. Make sure the loop is pointing down away from the tassel head. **(8)**

9. Place your thumb on top of this loop and hold down firmly to keep the loop in place. Lay the short tail of the thread to the top left-hand side of the tassel. Let it dangle down. Take the longer length of the cord in your hand and pull so the thread is well tensioned. **(9)**

10. Bring the long thread over the tassel to the left-hand side. Wrap the thread around the tassel head five times in a clockwise direction, directly in front of the paper wrapper. Keep this thread tightly tensioned while wrapping. **(10)**

11. Remove your thumb from the loop. Take the thread just used for wrapping the tassel head. Pass this thread through the loop so it runs down the length of the tassel. This end will become part of the tassel skirt. Pull on the top thread (nonwrapping thread) in an upward direction to pull through the loop. When the loop has disappeared, pull tightly on the top thread to secure. **(11a, 11b)**

12. Slide the wrapper down the length of the tassel until it reaches the desired tassel length. Using sharp scissors, make one cut across the tassel, directly below the bottom of the wrapper. Remove the wrapper. Trim any untidy ends. **(12a, 12b)**

13. Take the top thread that you pulled on in step 11, and thread this through a wool needle. Pass the needle and thread through the loop at the top of the tassel head.

14. Turn the needle so it is facing downward. Pass the needle and thread underneath and through the wrapped section completely. Unthread the needle. Trim this length so it is the same length as the tassel skirt. **(13)**

15. Comb through the tassel skirt with your finger, or a metal dining fork to smooth out any kinks. Hang the tassel so it dangles freely. Using a steam iron, gently steam the tassel. Leave to hang for a few hours before using. **(14)**

TASSEL MAKING USING THE EMBROIDERY SKEIN METHOD

11a

11b

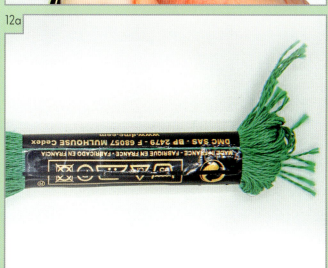
12a

12b

13

14

| 69

OFF-LOOM PASSEMENTERIE SKILLS

CORD SPINNING

The art of cord spinning is one of the foundational crafts of passementerie creation. In passementerie workshops, cords are handspun in a dazzling array of colors, yarns, and textures to create bespoke decorative wefts for weaving, tassel making, and rosette making. In my own work, I handspin the majority of the cords I weave with, as this enables me to create special, bespoke color, and material combinations that can't be found commercially.

In passementerie workshops, cords are spun in long, narrow rooms, using special equipment in a process that is very similar to rope making. A simple-to-use four-hook cord spinner makes the process of cord spinning at home accessible, simple, and fun! Any long lengths of yarn can be spun into a wonderful assortment of cord designs, both thick and thin, to then be used within your weaving projects. Cord winding is addictive, and you may find you enjoy it just as much as weaving passementerie!

If you don't have a four-hook cord spinner, simple cords can be made using the pencil-twisting method, or by adapting a handheld electric whisk with two beaters. Both these methods can work well, but they are not suitable to create long lengths of cord.

If you don't have a cord spinner, a wonderful range of ready-made cords can be purchased to be used as decorative weft. Please see page 32 for ready-made cord ideas.

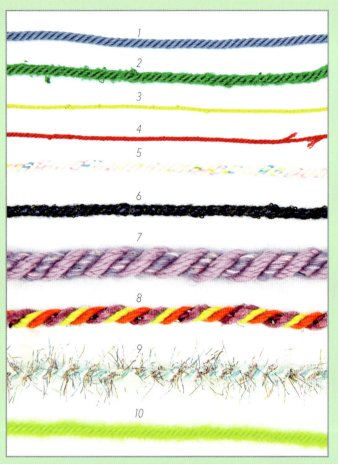

Handspun cords, *from top to bottom*:

1. 132 total strands of lace-weight mercerized cotton.
2. 16 total strands of Throwsters silk yarn.
3. 40 total strands of 2/60 nm slub silk yarn.
4. 16 total strands of 28/2 nm linen yarn.
5. 8 total strands of dip-dyed 100 percent wool light/DK yarn.
6. Combining different yarns in one cord—Lurex, 100 percent merino wool superfine/sock-weight yarn, and sequin yarn.
7. Combining bulky/chunky merino/alpaca yarn, lace-weight mohair, and 100 percent merino wool sock-weight yarn.
8. Combining recycled sari silk yarn, chenille yarn, and chunky merino/alpaca yarn.
9. Fancy cord—combining tinsel yarn, bulky/chunky wool, and fringed yarn.
10. 24 strands total of lace-weight silk mohair yarn.

CORD SPINNING

Handspun cords from leftover yarns and fabrics
Cord spinning can be a great way to use leftover yarns from other craft projects, transforming scraps into something both beautiful and useful. These shorter cords can be used to create the Scallop napkin rings and the Patchwork cuff bracelet projects. You could also use these cords as tassel-hanging cords or for all manner of embroidery projects.

1. Sixteen strands in total. Cord made from light/DK and lace-weight mohair scraps. These were short pieces that I tied together to create one continuous length, which results in a color change effect throughout the length of the cord. If tying yarns together, make sure to trim back the knot tails; otherwise these will catch during the cord-making process. (1, 4)

2. Sixteen strands in total. This was made by using one length of yarn at a time. Each end of yarn was tied off at the out end. A fresh yarn in a different color or texture was tied onto the out end, stretched back to the cord winder, and tied off. (2, 5)

3. Four ½ in. (1.2 cm) wide strips were cut from a damaged vintage mohair scarf and tied individually to each cord winder hook and each out-end hook. Two lengths of light/DK wool yarn and two lengths of lace-weight mohair/silk yarn were tied individually to each hook, on top of the scarf strips. This has resulted in a fabulous, fringy, tweed-effect cord. (3, 6)

| 71

OFF-LOOM PASSEMENTERIE SKILLS

Equipment
1. Four-hook cord spinner.
2. Cord spinner holder.
3. Four-hook cup hook out end.
4. 2 metal G-clamps.
5. Measuring tape.
6. Sharp scissors.
7. Clear adhesive tape (optional).
8. Table for creating small lengths and test cords.
9. A long room (or the garden on a good day), for creating long continuous lengths. If you are making a long length (over 3.2 yd. (3 m), it is useful to have an extra pair of hands to help manage the length.

Materials
Any type of yarn that is supplied in long, continuous lengths is ideal for cord spinning. Yarns that are available on a cone or bobbin are ideal for cord spinning, as these are a managed way of dealing with continuous lengths of yarn. Each different type of fiber, as well as the thickness of the yarn, will affect the end handle and sculptural abilities of the cords.

For example, a handspun thick wool cord will behave very differently from a cord spun from thin, delicate silk. A lot of cord spinning, even for me, is about trial and error. I encourage you to explore various combinations of yarns (and keep good notes) to see what results you can achieve.

Method
For demonstration purposes, the step-by-step instructions below show how to make a shorter length of cord. The process of creating longer lengths is exactly the same as detailed below, with a few extra considerations—see the following section for details on longer lengths.

Calculate how long you would like your finished cord to be, taking into account that you will lose approximately 15 percent of the total cord length through the spinning process. For example, to make a cord with a final spun length of 39 in. (100 cm), calculate

- 39 in. + 5.8 in. (15 percent of 39 in.) = 44.8 in.
  (100 cm + 14.7 cm (15 percent of 14.7 cm) = 114.7 cm).

This means that you will need to set up your cord winder on a table with a space of at least 44.8 in. (114.7 cm) between the cord winder and the out end.

Calculating the quantity of yarn required

This can be challenging to work out. If in doubt, always buy more yarn than you think you will require. As an approximate calculation:

- Total length of cord required (including 15 percent take-up + extra 2 in. (5 cm) to allow hook take-up) × strands per hook × four hooks = total quantity of yarn required.

For example, to make a cord of 39 in. (100 cm) long, using four strands of cotton per hook:

1. 39 in. (100 cm) [total length required] + 5.8 in. (14.7 cm) [15 percent take-up] + 2 in. (5 cm) [hook allowance] = 47 in. (120 cm)
2. 47 in. (120 cm) × four [strands per hook] = 189 in. (480 cm)
3. 189 in. (480 cm) × 4 [four hooks used] = 755 in. (1,920 cm)
4. Round up 755 in. (1,920 cm) to 800 in. (2,000 cm)
5. = 21.8 yd. (20 m) in total needed to make the above cord.

Setup to create a 16-strand cord from lace-weight mercerized cotton

Always keep the quantity of strands the same for each hook.

1. Measure out the space required for the cord. Attach the cord spinner holder to one end of the table with a G-clamp.
2. Attach the out end to the other end of the table with a G-clamp, with the cup hooks facing upward. Make sure the hooks of the out end and the hooks of the cord spinner are parallel to each other.

CORD SPINNING

OFF-LOOM PASSEMENTERIE SKILLS

1. Measure out 15 percent of the total distance between the cord spinner and the out end. Mark this 15 percent point on the table, directly in front of the cord spinner.
2. As you stand behind the cord spinner, tie the yarn in a double knot to the bottom left hook of the cord spinner. Ensure this knot is secure.
3. Using a medium tension, walk the yarn to the corresponding hook on the out end. Don't pull too tightly on the yarn, and don't allow the yarn to sag. Keep it taut.
4. Loop this yarn around the hook. You do not need to tie the yarn at this end.
5. Take the yarn back to the same hook on the cord spinner. Loop this yarn around the hook. Walk this yarn back to the same cup hook on the out end. Loop the yarn around the same hook previously used. **(1)**
6. Walk this yarn back to the same hook on the cord spinner and repeat the above walking process until you have four threads wrapped around the hooks.

    Very important tip—trim back any longer yarn tails; otherwise these will get caught in the cord-winding process and will cause irritating problems.

7. At the cord spinner end, keep the tension on the stretched-out yarn. Cut the yarn from the bobbin or cone, leaving a long tail. Take this tail and tie it around the group of four yarns. Repeat this same process until all the hooks contain four continuous strands of yarn. **(2, 3)**

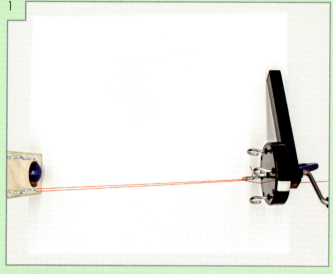

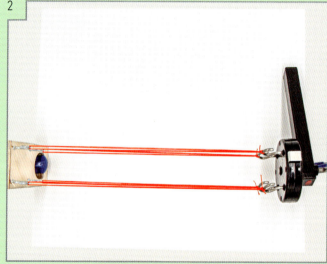

CORD SPINNING

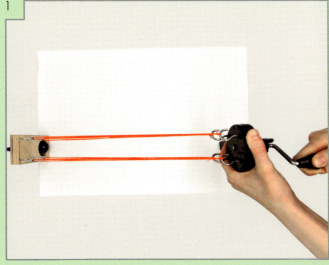

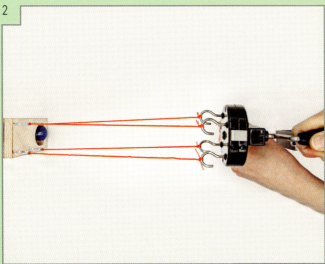

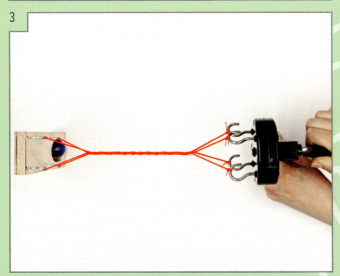

Spinning the cord

The cord needs to be spun in two stages. The first stage, the initial twist, involves tightly spinning the individual bunches of yarn together in their own groups in order to place tension through the yarns. Stage 2 involves tightly spinning these individual bunches together to create one cord.

1. Lift the cord spinner out of the holder, maintaining tension through the yarns.
2. Press and hold the silver button on the cord spinner. This locks the hooks in place, ensuring that the individual bunches of yarn are spun separately in their groupings, rather than all being spun together at once.
3. With your other hand, grip the cord spinner handle.
4. With the silver button held down, turn the handle in a clockwise direction. **(1)**
5. After a short time, you will feel the cord spinner pull toward the out end. As you feel this happen, allow the cord spinner to move toward the out end, maintaining the same tension as before through the yarns.
6. Keep twisting the yarns with the silver button pressed down. Stop twisting when you reach the 15 percent indicator mark on the table. Look closely at the yarns and you will notice that the bunches are now tightly spun together.
7. Release the silver button. Move your hand down to hold the long handle. Keep your other hand on the cord spinner handle. **(2)**
8. Continue to turn the handle in a clockwise direction. The individual bunches of yarn will now spin together. During this stage, you may feel the yarns lengthen back toward the cord spinner—this is normal. If this happens, maintain the tension while lengthening. **(3)**

| 75

OFF-LOOM PASSEMENTERIE SKILLS

9. Keep spinning until there is a gap of about 1 in. (2.5 cm) of yarn not spun between the top of the cord and the cord spinner. Don't spin any closer than this, as it can cause the cord spinner to break. **(4)**
10. Gently remove the cord from the cord spinner and tie the bunches together in a knot, making sure to maintain tension through the cord. Pull tightly on the knot to secure. **(5)**
11. Keep the tension on the cord while the cord is removed from the out end and the bunches of yarn are tied into a knot. Pull tightly on the knot to secure.
12. Let go of one end of the cord. The cord may have a lot of energy, and it may spin of its own accord. Let the cord use up its energy and stop spinning before you run your hand through the cord to smooth out any kinks.
13. Store the cord around a cardboard tube until ready to use.

Considerations for spinning long lengths of cord

To spin a long, continuous length of cord, a long room (or outdoors) is needed. You do not need to use a table—simply secure each end of the cord-spinning equipment separately. Make sure the cord spinner and out end are roughly the same height from the ground. When spinning long lengths of cord, the cord can become very lively and "wave" up and down, which will affect the end result of the cord. Have a willing friend stand halfway down the cord and cup their hands around the halfway point of the cord to prevent this "wave" from happening.

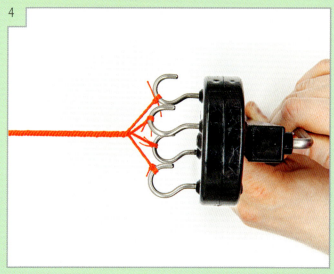

4

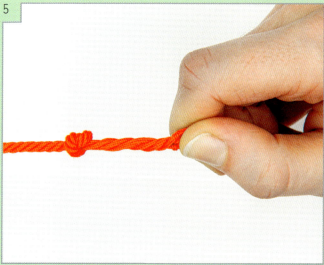

5

Combining different yarns together

Combining many different yarns within the same cord can give very exciting effects. Any combination of yarns, fabric strips, textures, and thicknesses can be combined within one cord. Care must be taken when spinning a cord made from different yarns, due to the difference in take-up between different types of yarn. When spinning together, some yarns may become very tight, while some may sag dramatically. Don't worry about this—ask a willing friend to stand behind the out end and pull any slack yarns so they are taut again while you carry on spinning as normal.

1

HOW TO MAKE FRINGE BUNCHES

Fringe can be made from any type of yarn—it just depends on what aesthetic you are aiming for. The fuller you make a fringe bunch, the thicker and fuller the resulting woven fringe will be. Follow the instructions below, using your choice of yarn.

Equipment
- Fringe posts, two points that yarn can be wrapped around: e.g., two secured wooden dowels or two cup hooks. I used a wooden dowel and a piece of wood into which cup hooks had been drilled.
- G-clamps, if needed to secure the two points to a table.
- Scissors.
- Yarn.

Method
The yarn is going to make a continuous loop around two points. This loop of yarn is often referred to as a hank of yarn. I used three yarns together to create my fringe bunches.

1. Set up your fringe-making station by securing the two points to the table. Leave a distance of approximately 24 in. (60 cm) between the two points. **(1)**
2. If using multiple strands of yarn to create a fringe bunch, tie the strands together. Tie the yarn securely around one of the fringe posts. **(2)**

2

OFF-LOOM PASSEMENTERIE SKILLS

3. Take the tied-on yarn and wrap it around the second fringe post, under light tension. Keep wrapping the yarn around the fringe posts to create a continuous loop of yarn. (3)
4. Continue wrapping the yarn until the bunch is the desired thickness for your project. To judge the thickness of the final fringe, look at half the bunch only. (4)
5. Remove one loop of fringe bunch from one fringe post. Cut through this loop and loosely tie both fringe ends. (5)
6. Remove the other end from the fringe post. Don't worry if the fringe bunch looks a little untidy—it can be combed through just before weaving. (6)

How to work out how much fringe you need

The easiest way to work this out is to weave a small sample of your design (around 10 in. / 25 cm), using the exact fringe materials you wish to use in the final design. Before you weave the sample, measure how much fringe you are starting with. Once the sample is woven, measure how much fringe you have left over and subtract this from how much fringe you started with. Now take this number and multiply by the length of the design you wish to create, adding an extra 10 percent to the length of fringe for contingency.

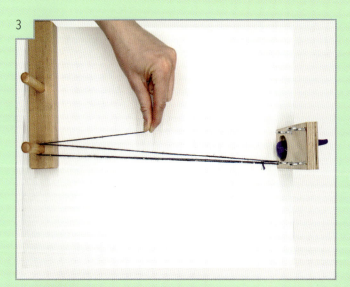

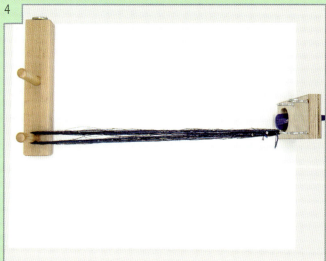

SQUARE KNOT BRAID VARIATION

This technique creates a textured, three-dimensional braid that works very well when used as a decorative weft or as a design feature in its own right. Any type of yarn can be used to create this square knot braid; however, tough and rigid yarns are best avoided if you are intending on using a braid for the decorative weft.

Materials and equipment
- Scissors.
- Strong adhesive tape.
- 3 strands of yarn, in different colors or one color.

A note on measurements
Calculate the length of braid required for your project and add an extra 15 percent to this final length for take-up. Measure out three separate pieces of yarn (*as above*), using this measurement.

Macramé terminology
- **Working lengths**: The lengths of yarn used to make knots.
- **Filler length**: The length of yarn that forms the middle of the braid. The working lengths wrap around the filler length to create knots.

Method
1. Tie the three strands in a knot at one end. Stick down the knot and yarn strands to the table, using adhesive tape. Separate each of the three strands. Ensure the middle strand (*shown in blue*) is vertical. Stick down this strand to the table approximately 8 in. (20 cm) from the knot at the top. This middle strand is called the filler length. (1)
2. Take the left-hand strand (*shown in orange*) and create a loop on top of the middle and right-hand strands. The tail of the left-hand strand will be horizontal over the two other yarns. (2)
3. Place the right-hand strand (*green*) on top of the of left-hand (*orange*) strand. (3)

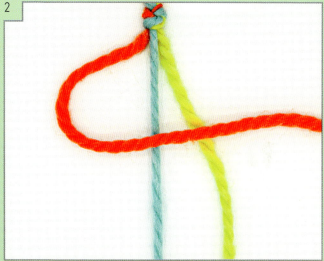

OFF-LOOM PASSEMENTERIE SKILLS

4. Pass the right-hand strand (*green*) underneath both the other strands and then guide into the loop on the left-hand side. (4)
5. Gently pull the strand through the loop. (5)
6. Gently pull on both horizontal lengths to close the loops. (6)
7. Continue to pull on the strands until they are snug around the middle strand. Push the knot that has been created up the middle strand until it sits at the top. (7)
8. Do the same thing in reverse, using what is now the right-hand strand (*orange*): create a loop and run the orange strand horizontally over the top of the middle strand. (8)
9. Place the left-hand strand (*green*) on top of the horizontal length and then guide it under both the other strands and the loop on the right-hand side. (9)
10. Gently tighten the knot and push it up the middle strand. (10)
11. Repeat steps 2–7 twice. This creates two square knots on the left-hand side of the filler knot.
12. Repeat steps 8–10 twice. This creates two square knots on the right-hand side of the filler knot.
13. Repeat steps 11–12 until the braid is the desired length. Knot the ends together. (11)

4

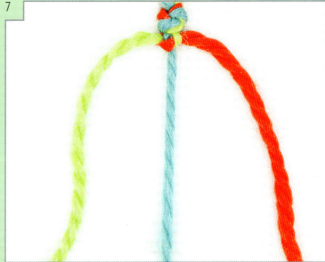

7

SQUARE KNOT BRAID VARIATION

OFF-LOOM PASSEMENTERIE SKILLS

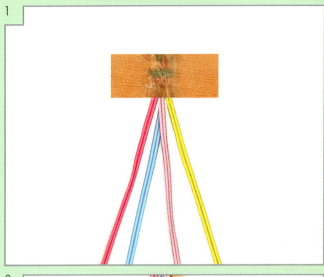

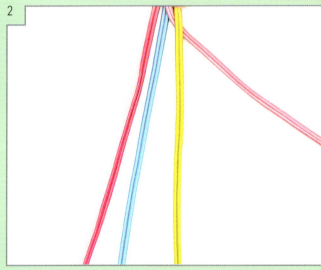

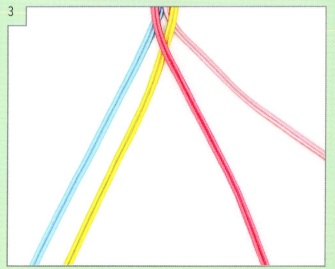

FOUR-STRAND PLAITING

This simple yet effective flat-plaiting technique creates a highly decorative length of material that you may like to use as your decorative weft. This plaiting technique can also be used as a passementerie design in its own right. It could be used as a decorative way of covering seams in upholstery or as an attractive trimming for jacket pocket edge decorations. This plaiting very quickly creates a long length.

Materials and equipment
- Scissors.
- Strong adhesive tape.
- 4 separate lengths of yarn, thin braid, thin cord, or another flexible material.

A note on measurements
Calculate the length of braid required for your project, and add an extra 15 percent to this final length for take-up. Measure out three separate pieces of yarn (*as above*), using this measurement.

Yarn and material choice for plaiting
If using a plait as a decorative weft, ensure you select a yarn or material that is soft and pliable to plait with. Using a rigid and tough material will create a hard and inflexible plait that will be difficult to weave with as decorative weft. The softer the material, the softer and more fluid the resulting plait will be.

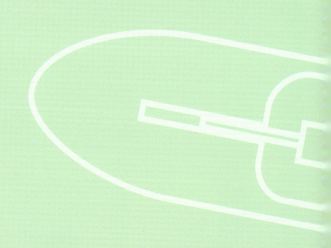

FOUR-STRAND PLAITING

Method

1. Tie your four strands in a knot at one end. Using adhesive tape, stick down the knot and cord ends to the table. Separate each of the four strands. (1)
2. Take the right-hand strand (*yellow*) and place it over and on top of its next-door neighbor (*light pink*). (2)
3. Take the first strand on the left (*bright pink*) and place it over and on top of the two strands to the right. (3)
4. Take the right-hand strand (*light pink*) and place it over and on top of its next-door neighbor (*bright pink*). (4)
5. Take the left strand (*blue*) and place it over and on top of the two strand to its right. (5)
6. Repeat steps 4–5 until the plait reaches the desired length. Tie the ends in a knot to secure.
7. The plait in various configurations. (6)

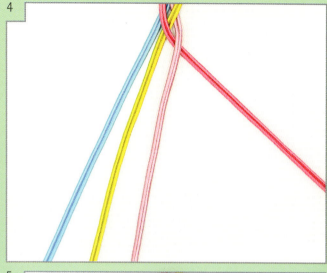

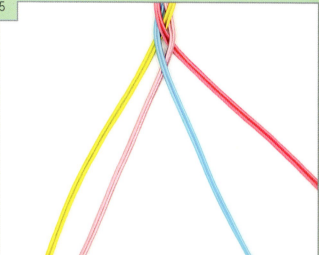

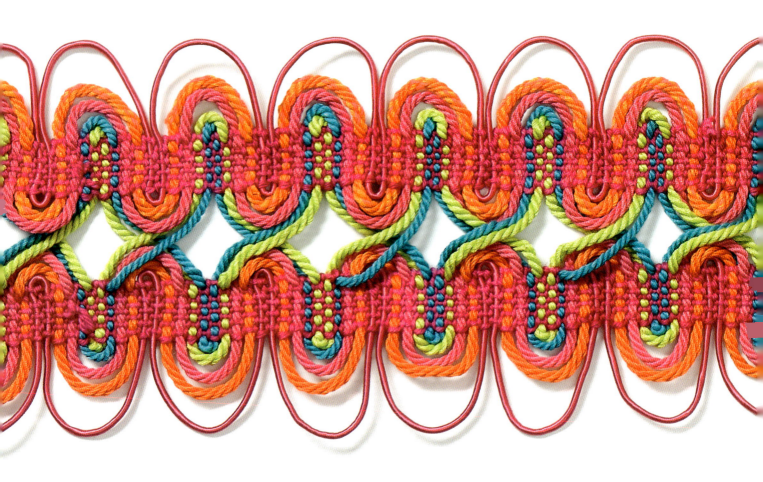

PROJECTS

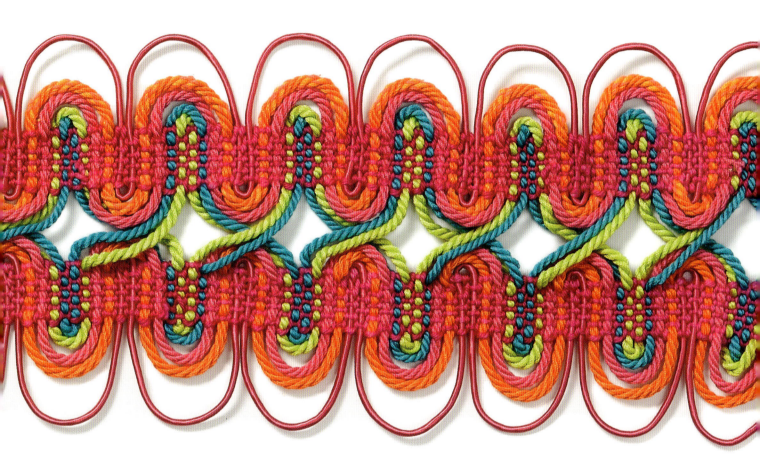

BOUCLÉ FANCY YARN CUFFS FOR A JACKET

A classic, colorful, spring tweed jacket is a staple in my wardrobe, and if you have one that could do with jazzing up, a great trick is to add removable handwoven fringes on the cuffs. The design has been inspired by traditional couture moss fringe designs, here reworked to suit contemporary fashion. This trim is made from a variety of playful materials in order to add a fun, yet chic, element to your garments. These fringed cuffs are attached to the jacket by using snap fasteners so that they can be removed quickly and easily for cleaning. This design could be woven in a longer length and in a variety of widths, to trim a hem, collar, or pocket edges.

This moss fringe uses minimal materials, which makes this a perfect stash-buster design. To design the colorway pictured here, I deliberately selected a range of green tones to coordinate well with the green jacket fabric without contrasting harshly. I've used a range of playfully textured yarns and materials that stop the design from looking flat and traditional when attached to the jacket.

Structural weft

This moss fringe incorporates a structural weft (SW), an ingenious passementerie weaving technique that is used to create stability within a fringed design. The SW is a smooth and strong weft yarn that weaves through the warp band in the same way as a main body weft. The use of a SW ensures that the edges of the warp are being held securely in place, which in turn supports the decorative fringed edges. If a fringed design is woven without a SW, it would immediately start to fall apart once removed from the tension of the loom. Use the same yarn as your warp for the SW.

Equipment
- Embroidery scissors (optional).
- Guide string yarn and guide string weights.
- Regular sharps needle.
- Rigid heddle loom or large frame loom.
- Scissors.
- Weaving shuttle or bobbins—one for fancy wefts and one for ribbons.
- 8 10 mm pairs of snap poppers.
- 15 ends to the inch dent.

Materials
Calculating the length of woven moss fringe needed
1. Lay your jacket flat on a table.
2. Measure around the diameter of the jacket cuffs. Make sure the tape measure is wrapped around the cuff snugly.
3. Make a note of this measurement. My jacket cuffs measure 10.5 in. (26.6 cm) long.
4. Take your measurement and add 2 in. (5 cm). The calculation is 10.5 in. (26.6 cm) + 2 in. (5 cm) = 12.5 in. (31.7 cm). This total measurement is how long the cuffs need to be, including a small seam allowance, and an allowance for shrinkage once the trim is removed from the loom.

PROJECTS

Materials to make two cuffs of 10.5 in. (26.6 cm)
- 25 g of light/DK 100 percent wool yarn—used here, ColorLab in Bottle Green from West Yorkshire Spinners.
- Polyester sewing thread to match the color of your garment.
- Two weighted guide strings. One guide string tied on ½ in. away from the left-hand warp selvage, and one guide string tied on ½ in. away from the right-hand warp selvage. For instructions on how to use guide strings, see page 52.
- Warp length 1.6 yd. (1.5 m).
- Warp sett: 8 warp ends, one warp end per reed dent, total warp width of ½ in. (1.3 cm).

Structural weft materials
- Light/DK 100 percent wool yarn, ColorLab in Bottle Green from West Yorkshire Spinners, wrapped around a bobbin.
- The structural weft (SW) is designed to blend into the background of the trim and should not be especially visible. You may wish to use the same yarn as the warp for the SW so the yarn blends into the background.

Fancy wefts (FW) for moss fringe
Fancy wefts one (FW1):
The below yarns (A, B, C, D) are plied together and wrapped around a shuttle or weaving bobbin. See page 45 for plying instructions.
A · 2 100 in. (254 cm) lengths of bright-green lace weight mohair—used here (*below*).
B · 2 100 in. (254 cm) lengths of teal lace-weight mohair.
C · 2 100 in. (254 cm) lengths of Scheepjes Sugar Rush mercerized cotton.
D · 1 100 in. (254 cm) length of 2 mm wide green velvet ribbon.

Fancy wefts two (FW2)
The three materials were wrapped around a yarn shuttle. Feel free to select your own exciting textured materials. The list below is just a suggestion of what you could use:
- 4.3 yd. (6 m) of 1 in. (2.5 cm) wide fringe ribbon.
- 4.3 yd. (6 m) of 4 mm dark-green ricrac ribbon.
- 4.3 yd. (6 m) of 4 mm green lace ribbon.

BOUCLÉ FANCY YARN CUFFS FOR A JACKET

WARP SETUP

1. Warp the loom with one warp of eight warp ends, with a total width of ½ in. (1.3 cm). Tie on securely to front beam stick.
2. Cut two separate lengths measuring 40 in. (102 cm) of strong, nonelastic yarn to be used as guide strings.
3. On the left-hand side of the warp band, thread the first guide string through an empty reed dent approximately ½ in. (1.3 cm) away from the first warp end.
4. On the right-hand side of the warp, repeat step 3 to tie on the right-hand guide string at a distance of approximately ½ in. (1.3 cm) from the last warp end.
5. Tie on each of the guide strings to the front beam stick.
6. At the back of the loom, tie each guide string onto a weight and leave hanging from the back beam of the loom. Ensure the weighted tension is tight.
7. Weave the ground ends through the warp only (imagine that the guide strings are not present). Using the structural weft (SW), weave 1 in. (2.5 cm) of plain weave.

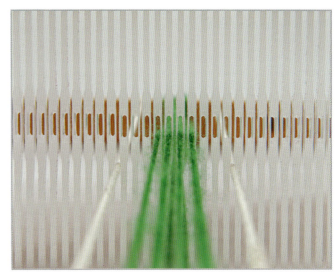

Guide string position in the reed.

Weaving the ground ends through the warp (see 7).

| 89

PROJECTS

WEAVING THE MOSS FRINGE

1. Using FW1, weave through the warp from left to right, leaving a ½ in. (1.3 cm) FW1 yarn tail on the left-hand side of the warp, on top of the left-hand guide string.
2. Weave FW1 from right to left, wrapping FW1 around the right-hand guide string. Make sure not to pull on the guide string as FW1 weaves through the warp. The guide strings must remain straight throughout the entire weaving process. (1)
3. Weave FW2 from left to right, leaving a ½ in. (1.3 cm) FW1 yarn tail on the left-hand side of the warp, on top of the left-hand guide string. (2)
4. Weave SW (*shown in purple*) left to right, leaving a 5 in. (13 cm) tail on the left (which will later be woven in with a needle and thread in the same way as MBW in other projects). The SW never weaves around either guide string. (3)
5. Weave SW right to left, making sure SW loop is snug around the right-hand side warp end. (4)
6. Weave FW2 from right to left, wrapping FW2 around the right-hand guide string. Make sure not to pull on the guide string as FW2 weaves through the warp. Weave SW left to right, making sure SW loop is snug around the left-hand side warp end. (5)
7. Repeat the design from steps 1–7 until the desired length has been achieved (6).
   When the moss fringe has reached the desired length, weave 1 in. (2.5 cm) of plain weave to finish.
8. When the first moss fringe is complete, weave a second length in the same way as the first.
9. Remove the moss fringe from the loom securely.

MAKING THE MOSS FRINGE INTO JACKET CUFFS

1. Once the weaving has been removed from the loom, gently pull out the guide strings. Weave in any weft tails and give the trims a tidy and a steam.
2. Prepare to separate the length of moss fringe into two separate lengths by securely fixing the area before it is cut (e.g., stitch-trim firmly or glue).
3. Cut into two separate lengths of moss fringe. You should have two lengths of fringe, bordered by plain-weave sections on either end of the fringe.
4. Steam both trims with a gentle iron to relax the fringe.
5. Pin down the moss fringe onto the jacket cuffs to check the position of the fringe. The plain-weave border sections should overlap on the underside of the jacket cuff, leaving only a small amount of plain weave visible. (7)
6. Sew snap poppers at regular intervals onto the jacket cuffs. If these cuffs are woven from heavy materials, you may need to attach more snap poppers to support the weight of the fringe. (8)
7. Sew the corresponding snap poppers onto the moss fringe, making sure that the positions of the snap poppers match up exactly to the positions of the snap poppers on the jacket cuffs. (9)

7

BOUCLÉ FANCY YARN CUFFS FOR A JACKET

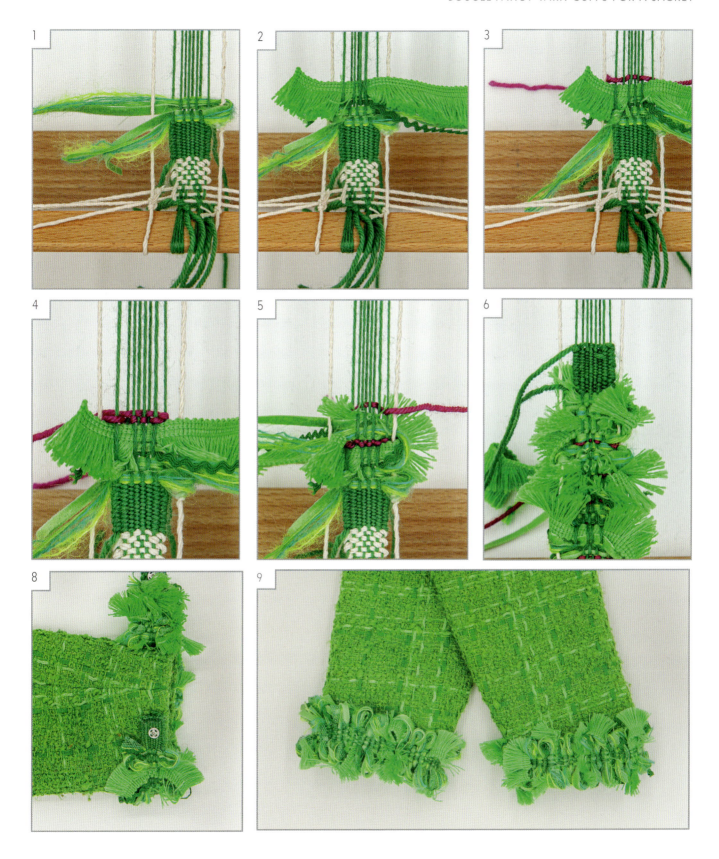

BEADED TASSEL FRINGE FOR A LAMPSHADE

This fabulous showstopper lampshade trimming is the icing on the cake. Designed to create a statement, this powerful punch of passementerie is a great way to liven up a lampshade you may have owned for years. This contemporary trimming design is created in two stages. It is woven using one main body weft and two decorative wefts. The beadwork and tassels are then attached to the trim once the design has been removed from the loom.

In my interpretation of this design, I devised a trim colorway to coordinate with the lampshade fabric, while not letting either element dominate. I have been careful to pick out the most-dominant colors from the fabric to use within my trim through the main body weft, the decorative wefts, tassels, and beads. You may like to create a trim colorway that coordinates well with your lampshade fabric, or you could create a bold contrast through using opposing colors or yarn textures.

If you are creating a trim for a small lampshade, simply adjust the width of the warp, the widths of the DW, and the length of the tassels to suit the size of the shade.

Equipment

- Cord spinner, if using.
- Embroidery scissors.
- Fabric scissors.
- Fine polyester sewing thread in a color to match bead selection.
- Fine polyester sewing thread in a color to work with MBW.
- Guide strings (optional).
- Pins.
- Regular sharps sewing needle.
- Rigid heddle loom.
- Size 15 reed.
- Tape measure.
- Yarn shuttle and bobbin.
- Beading needle.

Measurements

To weave a length to adorn the bottom of a 15.7 in. (40 cm) straight empire shade:

- Finished passementerie length is 53 in. (134 cm).
- Total woven width (minus tassels) = 2.5 in. (6.4 cm).
- Total width (including tassels) = 5¼ in. (13.7 cm).

PROJECTS

Materials

Warp yarn and length:
- 25 g light / La Bien Aimée Merino DK in "Sari" (enough for warp and MBW).
- Warp length needed: 2.7 yd. (2.5 m).
- Warp sett: eight warp ends, one warp end per reed dent, total warp width of ½ in. (1.3 cm).

Main body weft (MBW) yarn:
- 25 g light / La Bien Aimée Merino DK in "Sari," wound around a bobbin (enough for MBW and warp).

Decorative weft (DW) 1:
- 211 in. (5.4 m) of cord in color 1. I used a ¼ in. (0.6 cm) thick handspun cord made from Scheepjes Sweet Treat 100 percent cotton in Royal Orange.

Decorative weft (DW) 2:
- 211 in. (5.4 m) of cord in color 2. I used a ¼ in. (0.6 cm) thick handspun cord made from Scheepjes Sweet Treat 100 percent cotton in Delphinium.

Tassels:
- 20 skeins of DMC size 25 special embroidery thread. I used 10 skeins of color 3812 and 10 skeins of color 3850.

Beads:
- 100 4 mm beads. I used semitransparent crystal beads in orange and pink: 60 4 mm pink crystals and 40 4 mm orange crystals.

WARP SETUP

1. Warp the loom with one warp of eight warp ends, with a total width of ½ in. (3 cm). Tie on securely to the front beam stick.
2. Weave through ground ends.
3. Using MBW, weave 1 in. (2.5 cm) of plain weave.

WEAVING THE DESIGN

1. Weave DW1 through the warp right to left. Leave a short DW1 tail on the right-hand side of the warp. Weave four rows with MBW.
2. Weave DW2 through the warp right to left. Leave a short DW2 tail on the right-hand side of the warp. Weave four rows with MBW. **(1)**
3. Weave DW2 through warp left to right, creating a ½ in. (1.2 cm) picot on the left-hand side of the warp. Weave four rows with MBW. **(2)**
4. Weave DW1 through warp left to right, creating a 1¼ in. (3 cm) scallop on the left-hand side of the warp, around the DW2 picot. Weave eight rows with MBW. **(3)**
5. Weave DW1 through warp right to left, creating a ½ in. (1.2 cm) picot on the right-hand side of the warp. Weave four rows with MBW. **(4)**
6. Weave DW2 through warp right to left, creating a 1¼ in. (3 cm) scallop on the right-hand side of the warp around the DW1 picot. Weave four rows with MBW. **(5)**
7. Repeat steps 3–6 until the desired length has been woven. **(6)**
8. Using MBW, weave 1 in. (2.5 cm) of plain weave. Remove the weaving from the loom, making sure that the warp ends are secured well. Weave in weft tails and tidy up any messy areas. Lightly steam the passementerie length. Don't allow the iron bed to directly touch the trim.

BEADED TASSEL FRINGE FOR A LAMPSHADE

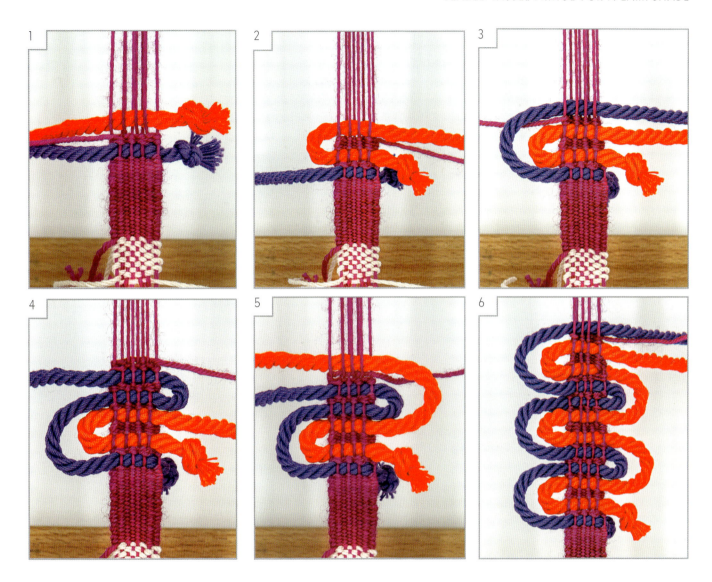

| 95

PROJECTS

ATTACHING TASSELS AND BEADS

Make 20 tassels, using the embroidery strand tassel-making technique (see page 66). These and the beads hang between every other DW1 scallop section. To attach them:

1. Cut 20 in. (51 cm) of polyester sewing thread. Thread the beading needle and pull the threaded length through the needle until both thread ends match. Tie both ends together in order to use two pieces of thread as one. Now thread the beading needle through the wrong side of the trim and secure well at the edge of the trim where you would like the beads and tassels to hang. **(7)**

2. Pass five beads onto the beading needle. **(8)**

3. Slide the beads down the beading needle and onto the sewing thread, then slide them down the length of the thread until the beads sit alongside the passementerie warp edge. Don't worry if the beads move around at this stage. **(9)**

4. Take a tassel in your hand. Pass the beading needle underneath the knotted hanging string, at the top of the tassel head. Pull the beading needle and sewing thread through this gap. **(10)**

5. Guide the tassel along the sewing thread until the tassel head sits alongside the beads. Leave a gap of around ¼ in. (6 mm) between the tassel head and the beads. **(11)**

6. Pass the beading needle and sewing thread back through each of the beads, working toward the trim edge. **(12)**

7. Once each of the beads has been threaded at the edge of the trim, gently pull through the thread to take up any unused length, until all the sewing thread is invisible. Don't pull too tightly on the thread, as this will create tension through the tassel heads and beads, which will result in a bunched-up appearance. The beads and tassels need to be able to hang freely from the edge of the trim. **(13)**

8. Once you are happy with the placement of the beads and tassels, knot and secure the sewing thread very firmly on the wrong side of the work. Trim off any thread tail. Trim off the hanging thread of the tassel, above the knot. **(14)**

9. Repeat step 1 until all the beads and tassels are attached. **(15)**

10. Gently steam-iron the trim and tassels.

BEADED TASSEL FRINGE FOR A LAMPSHADE

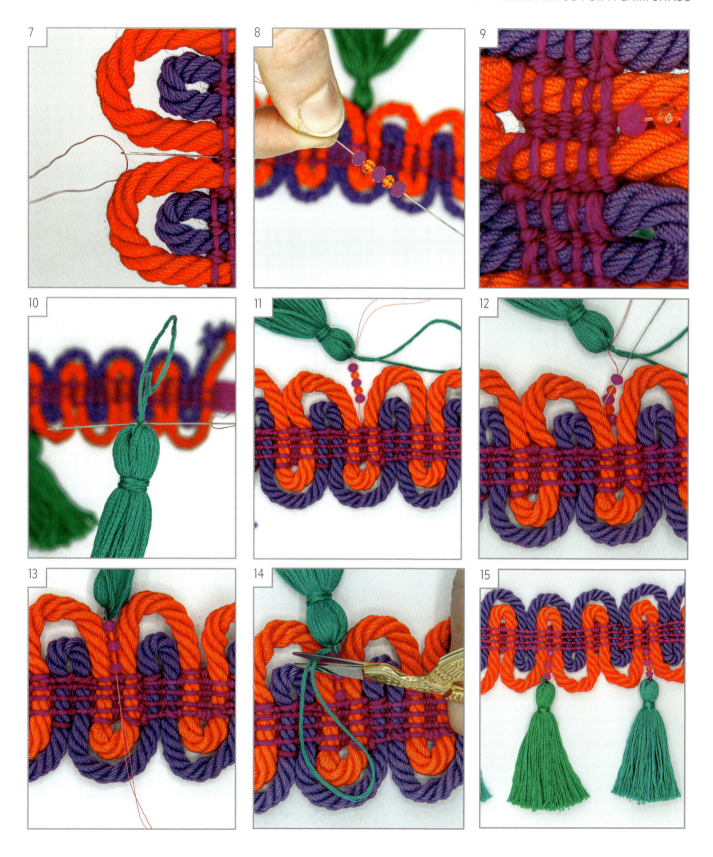

PROJECTS

ATTACHING THE TRIM TO THE LAMPSHADE

1. Identify where the lampshade fabric is joined together. This seam will become the back of the lampshade.
2. Take one end of the trimming and pin the plain-weave section to the lampshade edge. **(16)**
3. Working around the lampshade, pin the trim to the lampshade every 2 in. (5 cm).
4. Once all the trim has been pinned to the lampshade, check that it is sitting straight and even around the circumference of the shade. The top edge of the trim length should now be sitting straight around the lampshade rim. Pin the plain-weave warp ends neatly. **(17)**
5. Using polyester sewing thread and small running stitches, sew down the top edge of the trim to the shade. Use a thread color that blends in well with the color of the MBW. **(18)**
6. Continue to stitch down the trim length. Knot and tie off the sewing thread securely at the end of the trim. **(19)**
7. Gently steam the trim and lampshade, using a steam iron. Keep the iron around 4 in. (10 cm) away from the trim.

BEADED TASSEL FRINGE FOR A LAMPSHADE

DIP-DYED SHETLAND WOOL FRINGE

This textured fringe offers a delightfully contemporary contrast to the silky sheen of traditional handwoven fringes. Wool has always been used in passementerie weaving, and it was particularly popular in the sixteenth and seventeenth centuries.

Shetland wool is celebrated for its texture, strength, and natural rustic appeal. The Shetland wool yarn I used for this fringe has a delicious, crisp, full handle that fluffs up beautifully when dyed and washed, transforming into a bouncy, wild, and satisfying fringe. Depending on where you live in the world, you may be able to source beautiful locally produced wool yarn.

Dip-dyeing the edge of this trim in an intense pop of pink adds a fun and modern twist.

Handwoven fringes can be made from any type of yarn, and the following instructions will work for any yarn, so swap out the Shetland wool for a material of your choosing. If you are using a different yarn from the one listed here, you will need to adjust the thickness of your fringe bunches accordingly.

This fringe design uses an ingenious method for ensuring an even, straight-cut fringe. Two warps are used—one creates a header for the fringe, and the other, narrower warp holds the fringe in place while weaving. Once removed from the loom, this narrower warp is then cut off to reveal an even, straight fringe.

This dip-dyed fringe is perfect for adding a textural accent to any interior space. It would look spectacular trimming a chunky cushion, or edging the circumference of a lampshade.

Equipment
For dyeing:
- Apron.
- Dye bath—a deep stainless-steel pot is ideal.
- Dyeing utensils—teaspoon, plastic or metal serving spoon.
- Old bath towel.
- Rubber/synthetic gloves to protect your hands from the dye.
- Sink.
- Small jug or mug.
- Stove top/hob.

Weaving equipment:
- Rigid heddle loom.
- Scissors.
- Yarn shuttle or bobbin.
- 15 epi reed.

Materials and measurements
These make a 2 in. (5 cm) wide, 28 in. (71 cm) long wool fringe. When deciding on the length of your final trim, take into account shrinkage of the length caused by the dyeing process. Add an extra 3 in. (7.5 cm) to the final length to be on the safe side.

- 50 g of 2/6 nm (equivalent to a four-ply-weight yarn) Shetland wool for warp and weft yarn.
- **Warp length:** 1.6 yd. (1.5 m).
- **Warp sett:** This design uses two warps. The wider warp acts as the fringe header. The narrower warp holds the fringe bunches in place while weaving. When the fringe is removed from the loom, this narrow warp is cut off to create a straight, even-cut fringe length.
- Jacquard acid dyes in Hot Fuchsia (620) for dip-dyeing wool.
- White vinegar dye mordant.

PROJECTS

WARP SETUP

1. Warp the loom with one warp of 12 warp ends.
2. Sley the reed, putting one warp end through each dent until eight warp ends are threaded through the reed.
3. After the eighth warp end has been threaded, leave an empty gap in the reed of approximately 1¼ in. (3 cm). Sley the reed with the remaining four warp ends, putting one warp end through each dent.
4. Tie the warps securely to the front beam stick, making sure to keep the 1¼ in. (3 cm) gap between the warps. (1)
5. Weave the ground ends through both of the warps simultaneously. (2)

Structural weft (SW)

I used one length of pink wool wrapped around a bobbin as the structural weft. I used pink to show the SW clearly in the steps. In your own work, use one strand of fringe yarn as the SW. The structural weft is designed to blend into the background of the trim and should not be especially visible.

FRINGE BUNCHES

1. Make bunches of fringe as per the method on page 77.
2. To create this fringe, I used 10 individual strands of Shetland wool per fringe bunch. Each fringe bunch measures 100 in. (2.5 m). This is enough to weave approximately 7 in. (17.7 cm) of fringe.
3. Wrap the fringe bunch around a yarn shuttle.

Weaving the fringe

Make sure every row is woven into its own shed. You will find that this design needs a strong beat with the reed throughout the weaving process:

1. Weave ½ in. (1.2 cm) of plain weave on each warp band separately. Use two short lengths of the same yarn as your fringe. (3)
2. Weave one row of SW on each warp band separately, left to right, pictured here using pink yarn. (4)
3. Weave the fringe bunch through both warps left to right. The working length of the fringe will dangle from the right-hand narrow warp. (5)
4. Weave one row of SW on each warp band separately right to left, making sure the SW is snug around the right-hand warp end. (6)
5. Weave the fringe bunch through both warps right to left, creating a small picot around the right-hand warp edge. Weave through the SW on each warp separately.
6. Weave the fringe bunch through both warps left to right, creating a small picot around the left-hand warp edge. Weave through the SW on each warp separately.
7. Continue repeating the above steps, making sure to weave a row of SW after each fringe bunch has been woven. (7)
8. Make sure that the fringe picots on the left-hand edge of the left warp are roughly even and equal. It does not matter if the fringe picots on the right-hand edge of the right warp look untidy—these will be cut off when removed from the loom. (8)
9. At the end of the fringe design, weave ½ in. (1.2 cm) of plain weave with SW to finish the design.
10. Carefully remove the fringe from the loom. The warp ends need to be very secure to withstand the pressures of dyeing. Knot the ends very tightly.

DIP-DYED SHETLAND WOOL FRINGE

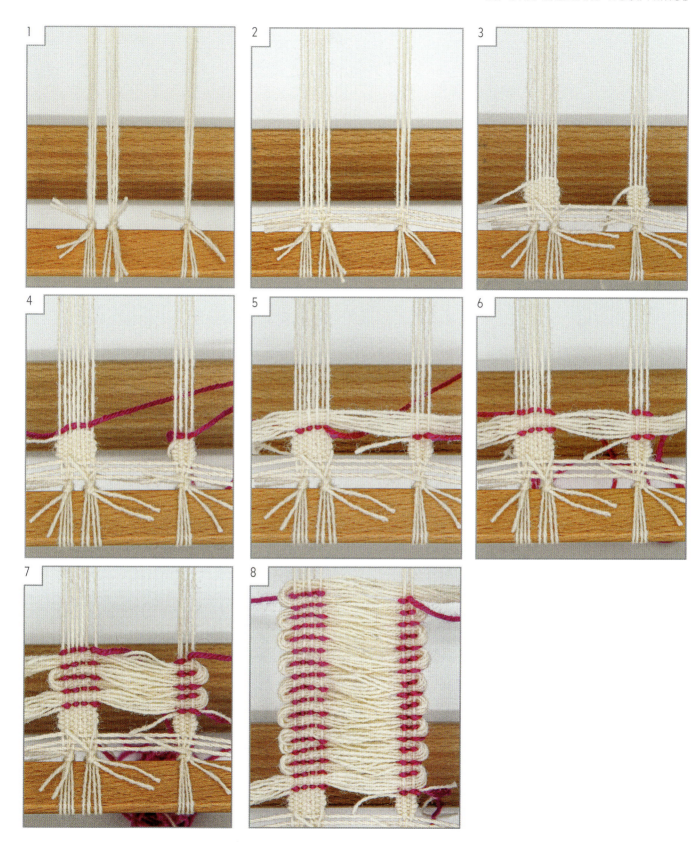

| 103

PROJECTS

Cutting the fringe

1. Gently steam-iron the fringe through a clean cloth on the reverse of the design.

2. Lay the fringe vertically, right side up, on the table in front of you, with the narrower warp on the right-hand side.

3. Using a very sharp pair of scissors, cut through the middle of the narrow warp. Follow the warp up the length, cutting the design straight until the right-hand narrow warp is removed completely. (9, 10)

DIP-DYEING YARN

Dip-dyeing yarn is a quick, simple, and fun process. The method given below is designed for dyeing wool yarn. If you are dyeing a plant-based yarn (e.g., cotton or linen), you will need to use a dye and a dyeing method that is different from the one listed below.

An acid dye is needed to dye wool yarn. Don't be put off by the "acid" in the name. It just means the dye needs to be used in conjunction with an acid (white vinegar) to adhere to the yarn correctly.

It is advisable to use specific equipment for dyeing—don't use the same pots and spoons you also use for cooking! Make sure to follow the health-and-safety advice supplied with your chosen dye.

1. Prepare the fringe for dyeing. Fill a sink or large bowl with warm water. Fully submerge the fringe into the water. You may need to agitate the fringe in the water in order to thoroughly soak it. Once it's thoroughly wetted, leave the fringe in the water bath (11, 12). To prepare the dye bath, half fill a deep, stainless-steel pan with warm water.

2. Place this saucepan on medium heat setting on the cooker top.

3. Half fill a small jug with hot water. Wearing gloves, dissolve half a teaspoonful of dye into the hot water. This will create a medium to strong dye bath. If you are dyeing a long length of fringe, more dye will be required. Mix well until all the dye has been dissolved. Keep wearing gloves until the dyeing process is complete.

4. Pour the dye solution into the pot on the cooker top and stir well until the dye solution is thoroughly mixed through. (13)

5. Add 5 tablespoons of white vinegar to the dye bath. Mix thoroughly.

6. Take the soaked fringe from the sink and gently squeeze out some of the water so the fringe is not dripping excessively.

7. Roll up the fringe neatly, ensuring the rolled-cut fringe edge is sitting evenly. Ensure the roll holds together well but is not rolled too tightly; otherwise the dye won't be able to penetrate the fibers. (14)

8. Do not let the dye bath boil or simmer. Light steam coming from the dye bath indicates that the water is the correct temperature. You do not want the liquid to become too hot—this can felt the fringe as well as burning your hands.

9. With the fringe rolled up, lower the bottom third of the bunch into the dye bath. Gently remove it from the bath, then lower it again to the same point. Repeat this raising-and-lowering sequence five times. This ensures the dye thoroughly permeates the fringe bunches. (15)

10. Hold the bunch steady in the bath for five minutes.

11. After five minutes, gently repeat the raising-and-lowering process from step 9.

12. Remove the fringe from the dye bath and put it into the empty sink. Run lukewarm water from the faucet across the fringe. Unroll the fringe bunch and wash it thoroughly, yet gently, in the water until no more dye bleeds from the fringe. (16)

13. Gently squeeze out excess water from the fringe. Lay it out on an old bath towel and roll the fringe and towel together. Lightly squeeze the length. Open out the roll (17).

14. To dry the fringe, move the length to a dry area of the bath towel. Keep the towel and fringe flat until dry.

15. Once dry, your fringe may need a trim and a gentle steam with an iron.

DIP-DYED SHETLAND WOOL FRINGE

DAHLIA BRAID FOR A CUSHION

This structural, curvaceous trim is based on a fabulous antique French trim in my collection. The color palette has been inspired by my favorite flower, the dahlia, which intrigues with its fresh and bold palette infused with delicate touches. In this project I used as MBW a gorgeous lace-weight, dip-dyed mohair that gradually changes color throughout its length. This design works especially well when woven using contrasting colors, as this heightens the effect of the scallops and picots.

Equipment

- Measuring tape.
- Material for guide strings (optional).
- Pins.
- Polyester sewing thread in a color that coordinates with the cushion and passementerie.
- Rigid heddle loom.
- Scissors.
- Weights for guide strings (optional).
- Weaving bobbin or shuttle.
- 15 epi reed.
- 22 × 22 in. (55 × 55 cm) cushion pad (using a larger cushion pad with a smaller cushion cover will ensure that your cushion looks plump and full).

Materials and measurements

- **Guide strings:** Optional
- **Reed:** 15 epi reed, one end per dent.
- **Warp yarn:** Strong, smooth light/DK yarn. I used yarn made from 50 percent merino wool and 50 percent silk.
- **Warp length:** 2.5 yd. (2.2 m).
- **Warp sett:** Eight ends in total to give a warp width of just under ¾ in. (1.9 cm).
- **Decorative wefts:** Select decorative wefts that hold their shape firmly when curved. The two decorative wefts pictured here are yellow wool and pink-wired gimp.
  1. DW1: Pink-wired gimp = 260 in. (7 m)
  2. DW2: Yellow wool = 364 in. (9.3 m)
- **Main body weft (MBW):** 40 g of seven-strand plied, dip-dyed, lace-weight mohair was used in this braid. See below for plying instructions.
- **Plying MBW weft yarn:** For this design I plied seven strands of lace-weight mohair together in order to create one thicker MBW.
  1. Cut seven long lengths of weft.
  2. Take each strand of yarn and then hold them together in your hand as one bunch.
  3. Wind this bunch around a yarn bobbin or yarn shuttle under a little tension, ensuring that each yarn winds around the bobbin/shuttle neatly.

PROJECTS

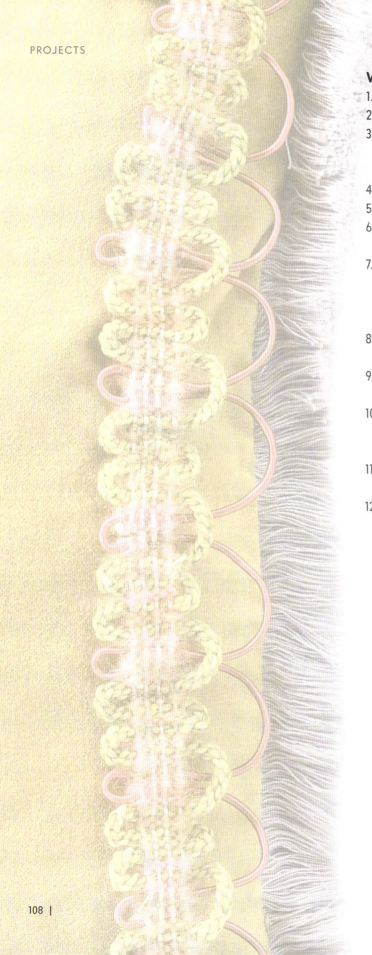

WARP SET UP

1. Warp the loom with one warp of eight warp ends in total.
2. Sley the rigid heddle with one warp end per dent.
3. Tie on the warp. Weave through the ground ends. Weave 2 in. (5 cm) plain weave with MBW. Beat down all rows of weaving really well to create a firm, stable design. **(1)**
4. Weave DW1 left to right. Weave three rows MBW. **(2)**
5. Weave DW2 right to left. Weave three rows MBW. **(3)**
6. Weave DW2 left to right, creating a ¼ in. (6 mm) picot on the left-hand side. Weave three rows MBW. **(4)**
7. Weave DW2 right to left, creating a ¼ in. (6 mm) picot on the right-hand side. Weave three rows MBW. Weave DW2 left to right, creating a ¼ in. (6 mm) picot on the left-hand side. Weave three rows MBW. **(5)**
8. Weave DW1 right to left, creating a 1 in. (2.5 cm) scallop on the right-hand side. Weave three rows MBW. **(6)**
9. Weave DW1 left to right, creating a ¼ in. (6 mm) picot on the left-hand side. Weave three rows MBW. **(7)**
10. Weave DW2 right to left, creating a ½ in. (1.2 cm) picot on the right-hand side that sits on top of DW1. Weave three rows MBW. **(8)**
11. Repeat design from steps 6 to 10 until trim is desired length, in this case 64 in. (162 cm). **(9)**
12. Finish design by weaving 2 in. (5 cm) plain weave with MBW. Remove securely from the loom. Once removed, finish ends securely with fabric glue or stitch. Gently steam-iron the trim, not letting the iron plate touch the trim.

DAHLIA BRAID FOR A CUSHION

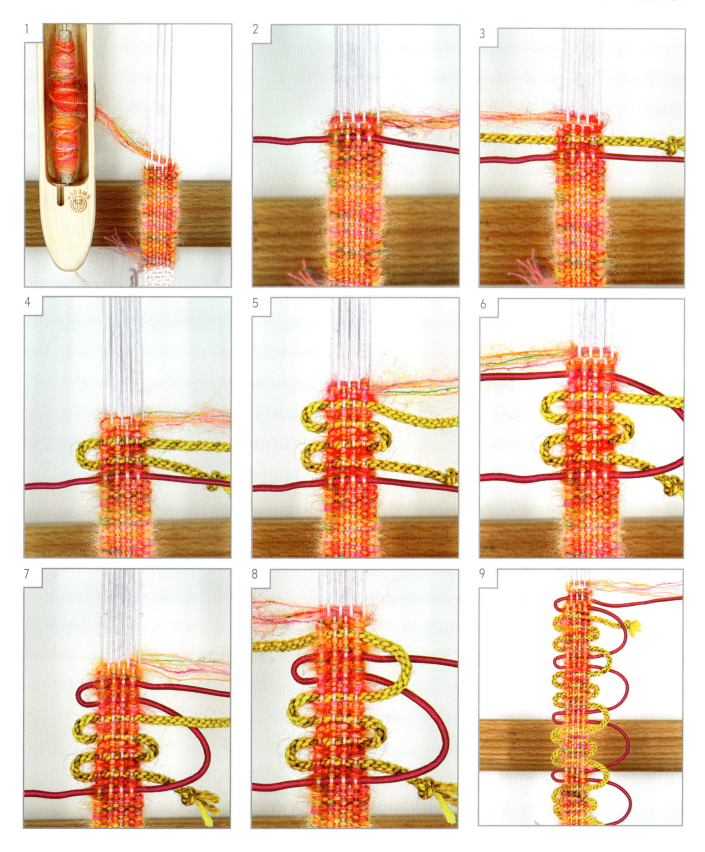

| 109

PROJECTS

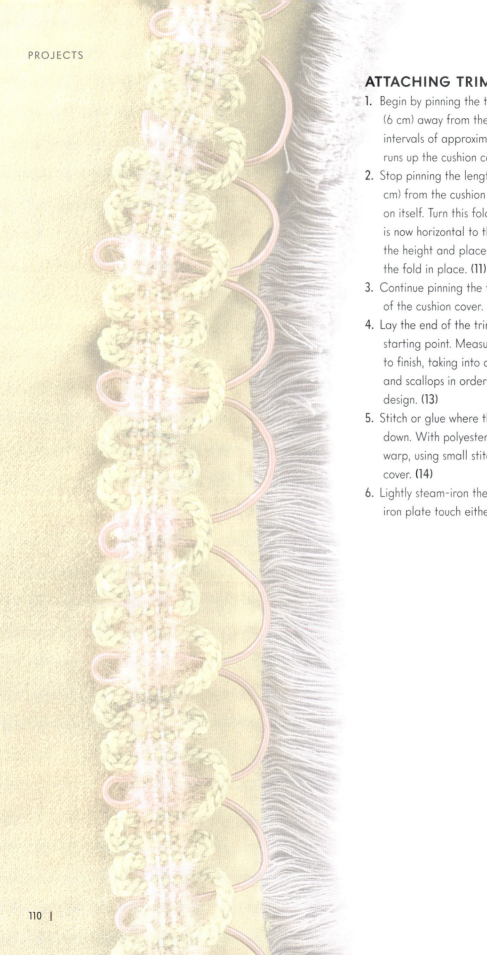

ATTACHING TRIM TO CUSHION COVER

1. Begin by pinning the trim to the cushion cover about 2.5 in. (6 cm) away from the edge of the cushion cover hem. Pin at intervals of approximately 3 in. (7.6 cm). Make sure the trim runs up the cushion cover straight. **(10)**

2. Stop pinning the length when the trim reaches about 5 in. (12.7 cm) from the cushion cover hem. Fold the length of trim back on itself. Turn this fold to the right-hand side so that the trim is now horizontal to the top edge of the cushion cover. Adjust the height and placement of the trim fold as required. Pin the fold in place. **(11)**

3. Continue pinning the trim length as above around each side of the cushion cover. **(12)**

4. Lay the end of the trim length directly on top of the pinned starting point. Measure where the end of the trim needs to finish, taking into account the placement of the picots and scallops in order to ensure the correct continuity of the design. **(13)**

5. Stitch or glue where the end needs to be cut. Pin this end down. With polyester sewing thread, sew up each side of the warp, using small stitches to secure the trim to the cushion cover. **(14)**

6. Lightly steam-iron the cushion cover and trim, not letting the iron plate touch either element.

DAHLIA BRAID FOR A CUSHION

10

11
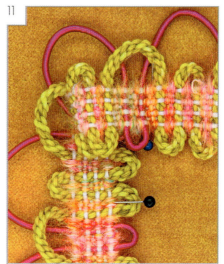

12

13
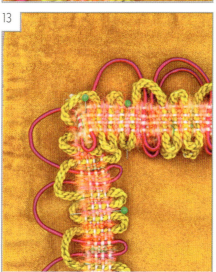

14

| 111

SCALLOP NAPKIN RINGS

A well-dressed table turns any meal into a special occasion. These napkin rings are quick to weave, yet they create a fabulous statement as part of a decorated table setting. Two separate warp bands are woven together on the loom and are joined by two separate decorative wefts. These napkin rings use very few materials, so they could be an ideal way to use up leftover materials from other projects.

The two warps are woven independently of each other, using two separate lengths of MBW. This design is held together by the decorative wefts, which travel through both warps at certain points.

The materials used here will withstand a gentle hand wash.

Equipment:
- Material for guide strings (optional)
- Measuring tape
- Pins
- Rigid heddle loom
- Scissors
- Weaving bobbin or shuttle
- Weights for guide strings (optional)
- Wool needle and a small length of MBW
- 15 epi reed

Materials and measurements

To make one 5.5 in. (14 cm) napkin ring:
- **Guide strings:** Optional
- **Reed:** 15 epi rigid heddle, with one warp end per dent. Between the two warps, a ¾ in. (2 cm) empty gap in the rigid heddle has been left
- **Warp yarn:** Light/DK 100 percent wool yarn. I used Weepaca yarn in Blue Eyes by Big Bad Wool.
- **Warp length:** 1 yd. (1 m). Even though the napkin ring is only 5.5 in. (14 cm) long, if putting on a warp just for this project, it is advisable to make the warp much longer than the finished project.
- **Warp sett:** This project requires two separate warps of four warp ends per warp.
- **Decorative wefts:** Two of 36 in. (91 cm) each. Select decorative wefts that hold their shape extremely well when curved.
  1. DW1: Handspun Scheepjes Sugar Rush cotton, eight strands per cord winding hook.
  2. DW2: Handspun Scheepjes Sugar Rush cotton, eight strands per cord winding hook.
- **Main body weft (MBW):** Same as warp. Two separate lengths of MBW are required—one to weave each warp.

| 113

PROJECTS

WARP SETUP

1. Warp the loom with one warp of eight ends in total.
2. Sley the rigid heddle with four warp ends, with one warp end per dent.
3. Next to the last warp end, leave an empty gap in the rigid heddle of ¾ in. (2 cm).
4. Sley the rigid heddle with the remaining four warp ends, with one warp end per dent, approximately ¾ in. (2 cm) away from the last warp end of the first warp.
5. Tie the two warps onto the front beam stick, keeping the ¾ in. (2 cm) distance between the warps. (1)

WEAVING THE NAPKIN RING

1. Weave through the ground ends. Weave 1 in. (2.5 cm) plain weave with MBW on each warp separately. Beat down all rows of weaving really well to create a firm, stable design. Weave through DW1 from right to left. Weave four rows MBW on each warp separately. (2)
2. Weave through DW2 from right to left. Weave four rows MBW. (3)
3. Weave through DW2 from left to right, creating a ½ in. (1 cm) picot on the left-hand side. Weave four rows MBW. Weave through DW1 from left to right, creating a ¾ in. (1.5 cm) scallop on the left-hand side around DW2 picot. Weave four rows MBW. (4)
4. Weave DW1 from right to left, creating a ½ in. (1 cm) picot on the right-hand side. Weave four rows MBW. Weave DW2 from right to left, creating a ¾ in. (1.5 cm) scallop on the right-hand side. Weave four rows MBW. (5)
5. Repeat steps 3–4 twice more until there are three repeats woven. Weave 1 in. (2.5 cm) plain weave with MBW. Remove trim securely from the loom. Finish the ends as required. (6)

SCALLOP NAPKIN RINGS

1

2

3
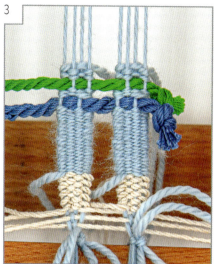

4
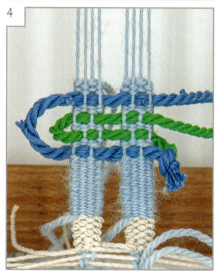

5
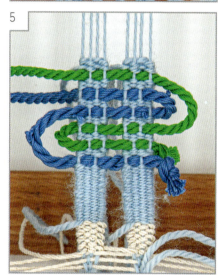

6
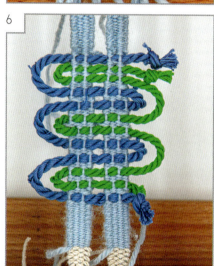

| 115

PROJECTS

MAKING UP INSTRUCTIONS

1. Roll the napkin in a way that replicates how the napkin ring would hold the napkin. Pin the trim around the napkin, overlapping the plain-weave borders. Pin both sides of the trim together. Check the placement and size of the napkin ring. **(7)**
2. Keeping the pins in place, stitch both ends of the napkin ring together, using a wool needle and MBW. **(8)**
3. Final napkin ring. **(9)**
4. Extra napkins rings showing the blue design and a pink colorway. **(10)**

SCALLOP NAPKIN RINGS

7

8

9

10

| 117

CORD-EDGED TASSEL CUSHION

The art of cord spinning shines brightly in this cord-bordered cushion. Here a variety of wool yarns in different textures and colors have been combined within one cord to create a highly tactile mélange cord. This project is a fantastic way to add an exciting update to a cushion you may already own. If you don't have a cord spinner, you could explore twisting yarns with a pencil, or source fabulous ready-made vintage cords to stitch around the cushion edge.

Cord spinning can also be a great way to make your own custom piping—simply stitch the finished cord to bias tape.

Tassels are the icing on the cake, and on page 66 you will find instructions to make a simple tassel, using an ingenious, fast method. Attached to the cushion corners, tassels add a tactile and fun embellishment. Only four tassels are used here, but you could increase the quantity to create an even more luxurious design.

Equipment
- Cord spinner.
- Pins.
- Regular sharps sewing needle.
- Scissors.

Materials and measurements
To edge a 19½ × 19½ in. (50 × 50 cm) cushion:
- 19½ × 19½ in. (50 × 50 cm) cushion cover.
- 21½ × 21½ in. (55 × 55 cm) cushion pad (using a larger cushion pad with a smaller cushion cover will ensure that your cushion looks plump and full).
- Four skeins of DMC size 25 special embroidery thread.
- 100 in. (254 cm) of cord, around ¾ in. (2 cm) diameter cord.
- Polyester sewing thread, in a coordinating color with the cord and cushion cover.
- Polyester sewing thread, in a coordinating color with the tassels and cushion cover.

PROJECTS

HANDSPUN CORD CONFIGURATION

This cord has been made from a variety of different yarns spun together. I spun it as one continuous length—but this needs a long room, or even the garden on a nice day, to be able to spin one continuous length.

Materials
1. Light/Superwash 100 percent merino wool by Madeline Tosh in shade Mars in Retrograde.
2. Rowan Kidsik Haze mohair and silk yarn in shade Candy Girl.
3. Falkland Wool nylon yarn in Bell Heather by AMO yarn.
4. Tosh DK by Madeline Tosh in shade Pop Rocks.

Four-hook cord spinner setup
As you stand in front of the cord spinner:
5. Top left hook: 10 strands of Bell Heather.
6. Top right hook: 20 strands of Mars in Retrograde.
7. Bottom left hook: 20 strands of Mars in Retrograde.
8. Bottom right hook: 10 strands of Bell Heather, 10 strands of Candy Girl, 10 strands of Pop Rocks.

Preparation
1. Make four tassels, using the embroidery skein method on page 66.
2. If the ends of your cord are knotted, these knots need to be removed before attaching the cord to the cushion cover. If the knots are left on the cord, it is very hard to disguise them on the finished cushion.
3. To seal the cord ends, paint an approximately ½ in. (1 cm) wide line of fabric glue around both of the cord ends, directly above the location of the knots. Let this glue dry completely. Once dry, cut off the knots, Cut through the majority of the fabric glue, leaving a line of glue approximately 3 mm wide behind on the cord. Lightly dab fabric glue on the cut end of the cord to seal the ends. Alternatively, the ends of the cords can be whipped. Please see page 154 on cord whipping, which can be found within the curtain tieback instructions.

Attaching the cord to the cushion
1. Iron out any creases in the cushion cover, then lay it flat on a table. If the cushion cover has a zip closure, make sure this is placed at the bottom before you start pinning the cord to the cover.
2. Attach the tassels to each cushion corner. Thread a regular sharps sewing needle with a long length of polyester thread. Knot the end of the thread. (1)
3. Place the needle and thread inside the cushion cover at the cushion corner. Secure the polyester thread by sewing through the cushion seam twice.
4. Pass the needle from the inside of the cushion cover to the outside, passing the needle between the cushion front and cushion back seam. Pull through the length of thread.
5. Thread the needle and thread through the hanging loop of the tassel.
6. Pass the needle back through the cushion corner seam from outside to inside. Pull through the length of thread until the top of the tassel-hanging cord sits flush to the cushion corner. Secure and tie off the sewing thread inside the cushion. Repeat until all four tassels are attached at the corners. (2)
7. Lay the cord around the flat cushion cover, pinning the cord to the cover while making sure to keep the attached tassels on top of the cord. (3)
8. Pin the entirety of the cord around the cover, ensuring that the start and end of the cord are at the bottom of the cushion cover.
9. Thread a regular sharps sewing needle with a long length of polyester sewing thread. Knot the end of the thread. Place the needle and thread inside the cushion cover at roughly the same location as the cord starting point (this point is on the outside of the cushion cover). Secure the polyester thread by sewing through the cushion seam twice.
10. Pass the needle from the inside of the cushion cover to the outside, passing the needle between the cushion front and cushion back seam. (4)
11. Pass the needle directly through the cord and pull through the entire length of thread. (5)

CORD-EDGED TASSEL CUSHION

12. Turn the needle and pass it back through the cord, making a small, almost invisible stitch through the cord. Pull the needle and length of thread through the cord to the inside of the cushion cover. Pull firmly on the thread to make sure it holds down the cord securely. **(6)**
13. Continue to sew down the cord, passing stitches through every 1 in. (2.5 cm).
14. If your cushion cover has a zip, ensure the cord is stitched down to the front side of the zip, rather than on top of the zip. At the end of the cord, knot and secure the thread securely.

| 121

JOSÉPHINE CRÊTE FOR A VELVET CUSHION

Inspired by historical designs seen at the Château de Versailles and reminiscent of the most-exquisite, classical eighteenth-century passementerie designs, this Joséphine crête is rendered thoroughly contemporary by the colors. Hot pink and chartreuse is my favorite color combination, and here I used this energetic palette to create a spectacular and opulent oversized design that looks magnificent trimming a velvet cushion.

Translated into English, *crête* means "ridge," and in this complex design there are many intricate interchanges between the four decorative wefts used, which creates the signature ridged crête appearance.

Applied to a complementary colored velvet cushion, this crête transforms a basic cushion into a sumptuous and luxurious interior artwork. You could weave many different versions and colorways of this design to create a lively and bold statement. Woven in a variety of scales and lengths, Joséphine could be used to adorn all manner of items from curtains to footstools.

Due to the many intricate interchanges between warp and weft, this design needs to be beaten down firmly with the reed throughout the duration of the weaving.

Equipment:
- Bobbins.
- Cord spinner, optional.
- Guide strings and guide string weights (if using).
- Measuring tape.
- Pins.
- Polyester sewing thread to blend in with each of the four DW.
- Polyester sewing thread to blend in with MBW and cushion color.
- Regular sharps sewing needle.
- Rigid heddle loom or large frame loom.
- 15 epi reed, one warp end per dent.

Materials and measurements

To make a 1.5 in. (3.8 cm) wide passementerie length to trim a 24 in. (60 cm) wide cushion:
- **Guide strings:** Optional, but can be very useful.
- **Warp yarn:** One 50 g ball of light/DK 100 percent wool yarn is plenty for the warp and main body weft (MBW). I used merino DK in Sari by La Bien Aimée for both warp and MBW.
- **Warp length:** 1.6 yd. (1.5 m).
- **Warp sett:** Twenty ends in total, one warp end per dent. Total warp width when reeded = 1.5 in. (3.8 cm).
- **Decorative wefts:** Four—three handspun cords and one bought gimp cord in this design. I handspun Scheepjes Sugar Rush cotton (four strands per cord-winding hook) to create the yellow-and-fuchsia cord. Then I handspun shocking-pink lace-weight mohair (six strands per hook). The fourth decorative weft is wired gimp cord. 73 in. (185 cm) of each decorative weft is required.

Tip: Consider the structural qualities of the proposed decorative wefts for this design. As the design is oversized, try to choose materials that hold their shape particularly well when creating scallops and picots, so that these elements don't droop when applied to an object.

PROJECTS

WARP SETUP

1. Warp the loom with one warp of twenty ends.
2. Sley the rigid heddle with one warp end per dent.

WEAVING THE DESIGN

1. Split the warp into two bunches of 10 warp ends. Tie each of these bunches around the front beam stick separately, but next to each other. Don't tie one bunch of twenty warp ends together, as this may result in the finished warp width becoming both significantly narrower and distorted, once the weaving begins. Weave through the ground ends. **(1)**
2. Weave 2 in. (5 cm) of plain weave, using MBW. Beat down well with the rigid heddle. **(2)**
3. Weave DW1 (*pink gimp*) right to left, leaving a ½ in. (1.2 cm) tail on the right-hand side of the warp. Using MBW, weave two rows and beat down well. Weave DW1 left to right, creating a ½ in. (1.2 cm) picot on the left-hand side of the warp. Weave two rows MBW. **(3)**
4. Weave DW2 (*yellow cord*) left to right. Weave two rows MBW. Weave DW2 right to left, creating a ½ in. (1.2 cm) picot on the right-hand side. Weave two rows MBW. **(4)**
5. Weave DW3 (*pink mohair*) right to left. Weave two rows MBW. Weave DW3 left to right, creating a ½ in. (1.2 cm) picot on the left-hand side. Weave two rows MBW. **(5)**
6. Weave DW4 (*pink cotton cord*) left to right. Weave two rows MBW. Weave DW4 right to left, creating a ½ in. (1.2 cm) picot on the right-hand side. Weave two rows MBW. **(6)**
7. Take DW1 and create a large scallop of 1.3 in. (3.5 cm) on the right-hand side. Weave DW1 right to left. Weave two rows MBW. Create a picot with DW1 on left-hand side. Weave two rows MBW. **(7)**
8. Weave DW2 left to right, creating a large scallop of 1.3 in. (3.5 cm) on the left-hand side. Weave two rows MBW. Weave DW2 right to left, creating a ½ in. (1.2 cm) picot on the right-hand side. Weave two rows MBW. **(8)**
9. Weave DW3 (*pink mohair*) right to left, creating a large scallop of 1.3 in. (3.5 cm) on the right-hand side. Weave two rows MBW. Weave DW3 left to right, creating a ½ in. (1.2 cm) picot on the left-hand side. Weave two rows MBW. **(9)**

JOSÉPHINE CRÊTE FOR A VELVET CUSHION

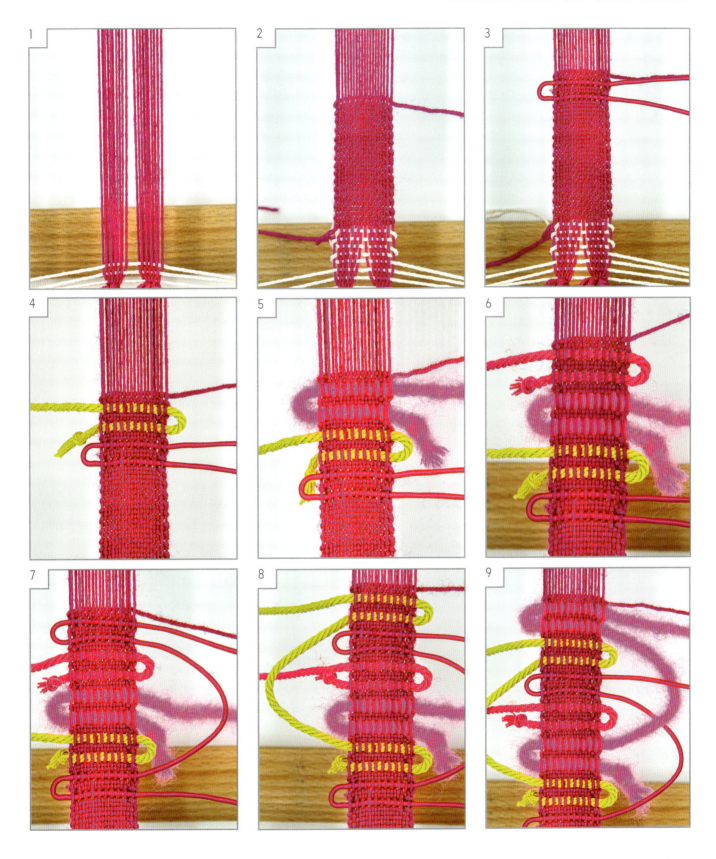

| 125

PROJECTS

10. Weave DW4 left to right, creating a large scallop of 1.3 in. (3.5 cm) on the left-hand side. Weave two rows MBW. Weave DW4 right to left, creating a ½ in. (1.2 cm) picot on the right-hand side. Weave two rows MBW. **(10)**

11. Repeat steps 9–12 until the desired length has been woven. **(11)**

12. As the weaving grows, ensure the design wraps around the front beam straight and even. Allow the design to build up directly on top of itself as it is wound around the front beam. **(12)**

13. When the desired length has been woven, weave 2 in. (5 cm) of plain weave, using MBW. Beat down well with the rigid heddle.

14. Remove securely from the loom. Gently guide out any guide strings, if you have used them. Weave in ends. Lightly steam your trim.

ATTACHING TO THE CUSHION

1. Lay your crête on top of your cushion to check the length of the design against the cushion top. You may need to remove some of the MBW border on each side. If you need to remove any length, ensure that the ends are secured extremely well before you cut.

2. Once happy with the length of your trim, pin the crête in place on the top side of the cushion cover. **(13)**

3. With polyester sewing thread, stitch along both selvages of the warp band. Use small stitches to secure the length of the trim to the cushion top.

4. Pin down scallops on either side of the warp. **(14)**

5. With polyester sewing thread to match each decorative weft, stitch over the halfway point of each scallop to secure the shape to the cushion. The picots are small enough that they should not need stitching down individually. **(15, 16)**

6. Each scallop is stitched down to the cushion. **(17)**

7. The finished cushion. **(18)**

JOSÉPHINE CRÊTE FOR A VELVET CUSHION

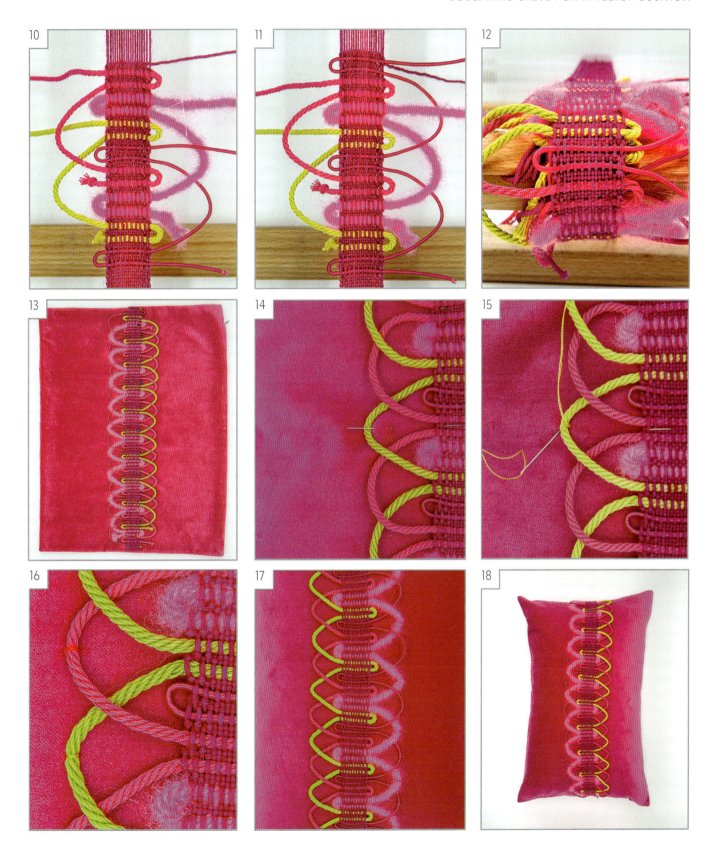

| 127

PATCHWORK CUFF BRACELET

When designing this cuff bracelet, I was inspired by the way that patchwork-quilt makers combine color and pattern together to create visually striking designs. Further influenced by the reuse of scrap textiles in patchwork quilts, I cord spun a colorful, textured cord by using scrap yarn left over from other projects.

This cuff bracelet is made using a variation of a passementerie design from the late 1700s that would have typically been used to decorate soft furnishings. Here, I played around with the scale, color, and application of the design to create a contemporary, yet classically inspired, cuff bracelet. This project is quick to create, so you could weave up a few versions in different colors and materials. This design hardly uses any warp, so it could be a great project to try if you have leftover warp on your loom.

Consider the materials carefully—make sure you use yarns and fibers that you are happy to have next to your skin.

Equipment:

- Bobbin or yarn shuttle.
- Cord spinner (optional).
- Fabric glue.
- Rigid heddle loom or large frame loom.
- Scissors.
- Yarn for guide strings (optional).
- 15 epi reed.
-

Bracelet:

- Epoxy glue.
- Jewelry pliers or long-nose pliers.
- ¾ in. (20 mm) ribbon crimp clamps with jump rings and chain attached.

Materials and measurements

To make a 6 in. (15.2 cm) long cuff bracelet. This bracelet uses a chain fastener that is fully adjustable in length to suit a range of wrist sizes.

- **Guide strings:** Optional
- **Warp yarn:** 100 percent wool light/DK yarn. I used La Bien Aimée merino DK in Sari.
- **Warp length:** This project requires only 9 in. (23 cm) of warp to weave the bracelet, plus another 6 in. (15.2 cm) of warp to take into account factors such as warp shrinkage and tension.
- **Warp sett:** Eight warp ends in total = roughly ¾ in. (1.9 cm) wide when set up.
- **Decorative wefts:** Two separate lengths, both 22 in. (65 cm) long. It is a good idea to select decorative wefts that hold their shape well. As this bracelet is designed to be worn, the design needs to have a tight, sculptural effect, rather than having floppy scallops and picots. I have used one DW made from wool and cotton yarn scraps (multicolored cord) and one made from Scheepjes Sugar Rush cotton. These cords differ dramatically in scale, to add further contrast to the design. You could use cords of the same weight, or two dramatically different scales, textures, or colors.
- **Main body weft:** Small amount of 100 percent wool light/DK yarn.

PROJECTS

WARP SETUP

1. Warp the loom with one warp of eight ends.
2. Sley the rigid heddle (15 epi reed) with one warp end per dent

WEAVING

The scallop and picot section is designed to fit around the wrist almost completely. There are two plain-weave borders at either end of the decorative section—these will eventually be trimmed down to size and the ribbon clamps added. For a longer length for a different wrist size, simply increase the amount of plain-weave border sections.

1. Using MBW, weave 2 in. (5 cm) of plain weave at the beginning (increase plain-weave quantity as required). Keep a firm beat throughout the weaving of this design. (1)
2. Weave DW1 (multicolored cord) right to left. Weave four rows MBW. (2)
3. Weave DW2 left to right. Weave four rows MBW. (3)
4. Weave DW2 right to left, creating a small picot of ¼ in. (6 mm) on the right. Weave four rows MBW. (4)
5. Weave DW2 left to right., creating a small picot of ¼ in. (6 mm) on the left-hand side. Weave four rows MBW. (5)
6. Weave DW2 right to left, creating a small picot of ¼ in. (6 mm) on the right. Weave four rows MBW. (6)
7. DW1 left to right, creating a scallop of 1 in. (2.5 cm) on the left-hand side. Weave four rows MBW. (7)
8. DW1 right to left, creating a picot on the right-hand side that is wider than DW2 picots. Weave four rows MBW. (8)
9. DW2 left to right, creating a scallop on the left-hand side that sits on top of DW1. Weave four rows MBW. (9)
10. Repeat steps 4–6, ending on a scallop on the left-hand side, using DW1. Using MBW, weave 2 in. (5 cm) of plain weave at the beginning (increase plain-weave quantity as required). (10)
11. Secure the ends well and remove from the loom. Lightly steam-iron the finished length.

PATCHWORK CUFF BRACELET

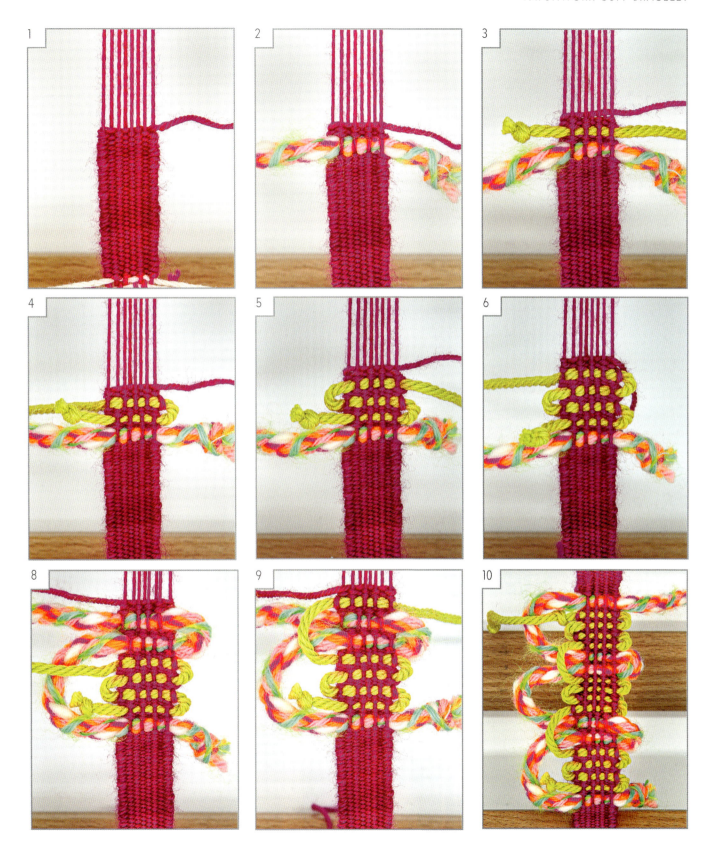

131

PROJECTS

MAKING THE BRACELET

1. Measure the finished length of your weaving on your wrist in order to judge how much plain weave to remove. Before cutting off the plain weave, make sure to glue or use a zigzag stitch across both warp ends to secure.
2. Using epoxy glue, run a thin line of glue inside one of the ribbon clamps. (1)
3. Guide the ribbon clamp onto one of the warp ends. Using pliers, press down across the width of the clamp tightly to secure. (2)
4. Repeat steps 2 and 3 with the second part of the ribbon clamp. (3)
5. Leave the bracelet to dry fully before weaving, ideally overnight. (4)

PATCHWORK CUFF BRACELET

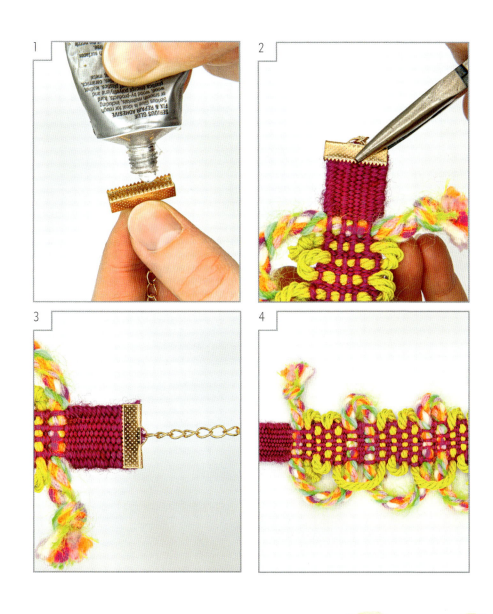

| 133

WISTERIA BORDER FOR A SCARF

The colors and materials of this chunky, squishy, oversized trim were inspired by a wisteria plant I saw ladened with blooms and foliage. The placement of the scallops and picots has been inspired by a tiny antique trim I have in my collection that measures only a diminutive ½ in. (12 mm) wide.

My version of the design embellishes a chunky scarf edge to maximum effect. At its widest point this design measures 5.5 in. (14 cm). I have also introduced a new technique to creating warps—fancy warp yarn overlay—to create a contemporary twist on traditional tweed fabrics. The passementerie is attached to the scarf by using snap poppers for easy removal for cleaning.

The materials and scale of the design can be easily changed to suit your tastes. Follow the weaving instructions below but simply change the width of the warp and the dimensions of the cords to suit your own project.

Equipment:

- Measuring tape
- Pins
- Polyester sewing thread in a color to coordinate with scarf and passementerie
- Rigid heddle loom or large frame loom
- Scissors
- Weaving bobbin or shuttle
- 15 epi reed
- 10 pairs of snap poppers.

Materials and measurements

- **Guide strings:** Optional.
- **Reed:** 15 epi reed, one end per dent.
- **Warp yarn:** 2 oz. (50 g) 100 percent superwash merino superfine/sock-weight yarn.
  Small amounts of fancy yarns in different colors and textures to create a yarn overlay (*see below*) in lengths no shorter than 2 yd. (2 m) continuous.
- **Warp length:** 2 yd. (2 m) to trim a scarf edge of 18 in. (46 cm).
- **Warp sett:** Twenty-two total ends, to give a total width of 2 in. (5 cm).
- **Decorative wefts:** Two chunky decorative wefts in opposing colors. I used 0.7 in. (2 cm) in diameter, made from a combination of chunky alpaca yarn, lace-weight mohair yarn, and superfine/sock-weight yarn, handspun on my cord spinner. This results in decorative wefts that hold their shape well, while still being soft and puffy to touch.
- **Main body weft (MBW):** Plied yarn made from two strands of superfine/sock-weight yarn and two strands of lace-weight mohair. See instructions below.
- **Plying MBW weft yarn** See page 45 for plying instructions. For this design, I plied four different-colored yarns together to create one thicker, multidimensional MBW. This creates a fun, multidimensional tweed effect when woven.

PROJECTS

WARP SETUP

Instructions for creating fancy warp overlay:

In order to create the fancy warp overlay, the loom is warped in two stages. First off, all the main base warp (superfine/sock-weight yarn) is added to the loom in the usual manner. Once the base warp yarn is stretched onto the loom, the fancy yarn overlay is then randomly tied onto the back loom stick and threaded through the rigid heddle. I used strands of chunky alpaca yarn and fine lace-weight mohair as my fancy overlay.

1. Warp the loom with 22 ends of superfine/sock-weight yarn. Remove the yarn from the warping peg and cut through the yarn loop. Do not wind your warp around the beam.
2. To create the fancy yarn warp overlay, take one length of fancy yarn (pictured here in chunky green alpaca) and tie it onto the back beam, where the superfine/sock-weight warp yarn is secured. Where you want to tie on the fancy yarn, gently push this yarn base to one side. (1)
3. Thread this length of fancy yarn through a slot/eye in the reed that already contains a warp yarn. Make sure that the yarn is running in a straight line from the back beam stick through the rigid heddle. Pull through the fancy yarn until the end reaches the end of the warp yarn at the front of the loom. (2)
4. Repeat this process, working across the width of the warp base until you have tied on the desired amount of fancy yarns. Tie on as many fancy yarns as you wish. However, if using very thick fancy materials, it is advisable to tie on fewer lengths and space the chunky fancy yarns farther apart from each other. (3)

5. Once the fancy yarns are tied on, hold the warp lengths firmly under tension while the warp is wound onto the back beam. You may need to comb out the warp with your hand at several stages to allow the fancy yarns to pass neatly through the rigid heddle.
6. Sley the reed as normal, except this time you will have some dents containing only one yarn, and some dents containing multiple yarns.
7. Split the warp into two even-sized bunches. Tie each of these bunches around the front beam stick separately, but next to each other. Don't tie the warp as one large bunch, as this will distort the warp width once the weaving begins. (4)

WEAVING

1. Weave through the ground ends. Due to the fancy yarns, the warp shed may need encouragement to open. When the shed is open, lightly place your hand between the shed and comb through the warp yarns.
2. If working with a fancy warp, weave 1 in. (2.5 cm) of plain weave with a strong yarn to start. This will help keep the layers of warp in check. (5)
3. Weave 5 in. (13 cm) with MBW.* (This design is bordered by plain weave. Add more plain weave if you require a longer border, or a shorter quantity of plain weave if you want to weave a longer amount of the passementerie design.) (6)
4. Tie the end of DW1 in a tight knot. Weave DW1 left to right. Beat down very well. Weave three rows MBW. (7)
5. Tie the end of DW2 in a tight knot. Weave DW2 left to right. Beat down very well. Weave three rows MBW. (8)
6. Weave DW2 right to left, creating a 1 in. (2.5 cm) picot on the right-hand side. Beat down very well. Weave three rows MBW. (9)

More than this length may be needed if the scarf you're weaving is planned to be longer than the one pictured here.

136 |

WISTERIA BORDER FOR A SCARF

PROJECTS

7. Weave DW1 right to left, creating a 2 in. (5 cm) scallop on the right-hand side around the DW2 picot. Beat down very well. Weave three rows MBW. (10)
8. Weave DW1 left to right, creating a 1 in. (2.5 cm) picot on the left-hand side. Beat down very well. Weave three rows MBW.
9. Weave DW1 right to left, creating a 1 in. (2.5 cm) picot on the right-hand side. Beat down very well. Weave three rows MBW.
10. Weave DW1 left to right, creating a 1 in. (2.5 cm) picot on the left-hand side. Beat down very well. Weave three rows MBW. (11)
11. Weave DW2 left to right, creating a 3 in. (7.6 cm) scallop on the left-hand side. Beat down very well. Weave three rows MBW. (12)
12. Repeat steps 3–9 until desired length has been woven.
13. Weave 5 in. (13 cm)* with plied MBW to finish.
14. Remove the weaving securely from the loom.
15. Weave in weft tails. Secure warp ends, using fabric glue or stitch.
16. Give the trim a gentle steam iron to relax the warp and the fibers.

ATTACHING TO THE SCARF

1. Lay the scarf flat on a table. Lay the passementerie on top of the scarf along the edge, so the scallop and picot section is sitting directly central. Pin down one end of passementerie to the scarf. (13)
2. Fold back the passementerie, keeping one end pinned in place. Position the snap poppers to support the weight of the passementerie. If your trim is heavy, you may need to use more snap poppers. Stitch the poppers in place onto the scarf. Remove the pin. Stitch the other half of the snap poppers to the wrong side of the passementerie, making sure to position the snap poppers to align with the poppers on the scarf. (14)
3. Popper the passementerie to the scarf. Fold the plain-weave borders around so they are on the back of the scarf. Attach poppers to hold in place. (15)
4. Gently steam-iron.

* More than this length may be needed if the scarf you're weaving is planned to be longer than the one pictured here.

WISTERIA BORDER FOR A SCARF

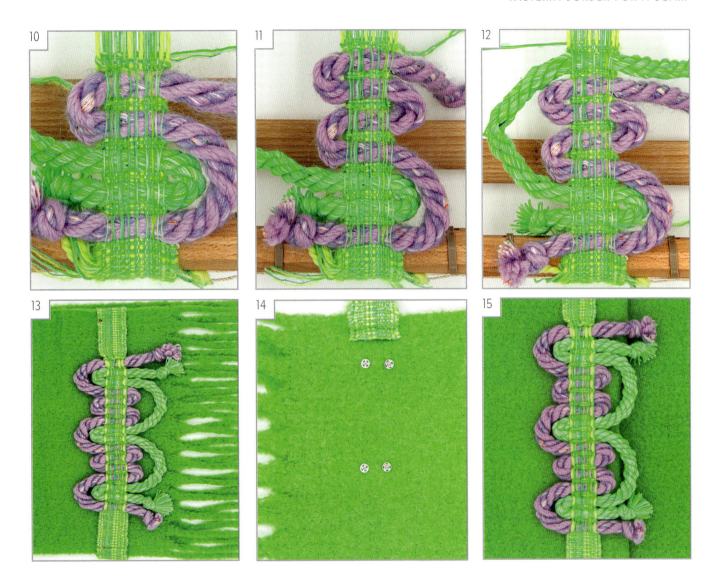

MARGOT CRÊTE FRINGE FOR A VELVET FOOTSTOOL

Glamorous yet playful, the Margot fringe is one of the most time consuming and challenging of the projects in this book. Festooned with a luxurious, sequinned, metallic fringe, this passementerie design opulently trims a velvet footstool. Taking inspiration from glamorous fringes of the 1800s and 1920s, this design exudes characterful decadence with a dash of eccentricity.

This fringe comprises two distinct parts, and it is created in the traditional manner of complex fringes. The first stage is to weave a long length of the crête design—called the header. The second stage is to weave a long length of plain fringe. The third stage is to stitch these two distinct sections together, so they appear as one unified design.

I used very fine yarns to create this fringe, which will give a traditional passementerie appearance. Working with fine yarns gives a beautiful effect; however, fine yarns are extremely time consuming to weave. Feel free to use different yarns from the ones suggested below—the thicker the yarn used, the thicker the bunch of yarn used, and the fuller and less fluid the fringe will look. I encourage you to pop a test warp on your loom to explore how different yarns behave as a fringe.

Equipment (for step 1 and step 2)
- Cord spinner and equipment (optional).
- Fringe-making equipment (see page 77).
- Ground end yarn.
- Material for guide strings (optional).
- Measuring tape.
- Pins.
- Rigid heddle loom.
- Scissors.
- Weaving bobbin or shuttle.
- Weights for guide strings (optional).
- 15 epi reed.

Materials and measurements
Measuring the footstool:
1. Measure the circumference of the footstool. The footstool pictured here has a circumference of 51 in. (130 cm).
2. Add an extra 6 in. (15 cm) to this circumference length (to account for the plain-weave border on either end of the trim and tension take-up) = 57 in. (144 cm).

Crête header:
To make a continuous length of passementerie measuring 57 in. (144 cm)
- **Guide strings:** Optional.
- **Reed:** One end per dent.
- **Warp yarn:** 100 percent wool light/DK knit yarn, shown here in blue.
- **Warp length:** 2.5 yd. (2.2 m).
- **Warp sett:** 15 epi rigid heddle.
- **Decorative wefts:** Two decorative wefts in total.
- **DW1:** 26 ft. (8 m). Shown here is a handspun cord made from an assortment of yarns
- **DW2:** 26 ft. (8 m) × 4 mm double-faced velvet ribbon in midnight navy.
- **Main body weft (MBW):** One strand of light/DK wool yarn (same yarn used for warp), one strand of fine sequin yarn, and two strands of Lurex yarn, all plied together around a bobbin.

Fringe bunches:
See page 77 for how to make fringe bunches.

For the structural weft (SW) I used a range of yarns in subtly different colors within each fringe bunch, in order to create a multidimensional color effect. This prevents the fringe from looking flat.

Each bunch contains
- 30 strands of metallic blue Lurex yarn.
- 6 strands of fine, metallic sequin yarn.
- 15 bunches of fringe in total, to weave the fringe. Each fringe bunch measured 24 in. (61 cm).

| 141

PROJECTS

STEP 1: CRÊTE HEADER

WARPING INSTRUCTIONS
1. Warp the loom with a total of 12 warp ends. This will give a warp width of just under 1 in. (2.5 cm).
2. Sley the rigid heddle, putting one warp end per dent.

WEAVING INSTRUCTIONS
1. Weave through the ground ends. Weave 2 in. (5 cm) of plain weave with MBW. Beat down thoroughly and after all subsequent rows. **(1)**
2. Weave DW1 right to left. Weave four rows MBW. **(2)**
3. Weave DW2 right to left. Weave four rows MBW. **(3)**
4. Weave DW2 left to right, creating a ½ in. (1.2 cm) picot on the left-hand side. Explore how to shape the velvet—I folded the velvet ribbon to create a pleasing tightly folded effect. Weave four rows MBW. **(4)**
5. Weave DW1 left to right, creating a 1 in. (2.5 cm) scallop on the left-hand side around the DW2 picot. Weave four rows MBW. **(5)**
6. Weave DW1 right to left, creating a long picot measuring 1½ in. (3.8 cm). Weave four rows MBW. **(6)**
7. Weave DW2 right to left, creating a scallop measuring 1¾ in. (4.5 cm). This scallop is designed to halo around the picot created by DW1. Weave four rows MBW. **(7)**
8. Continue to repeat steps 4–6 until the trim is the desired length. **(8)**
9. Keep checking the selvages to make sure they are weaving straight and even.
10. Allow the length of trim to build up directly on top of itself around the front beam.

MARGOT CRÊTE FRINGE FOR A VELVET FOOTSTOOL

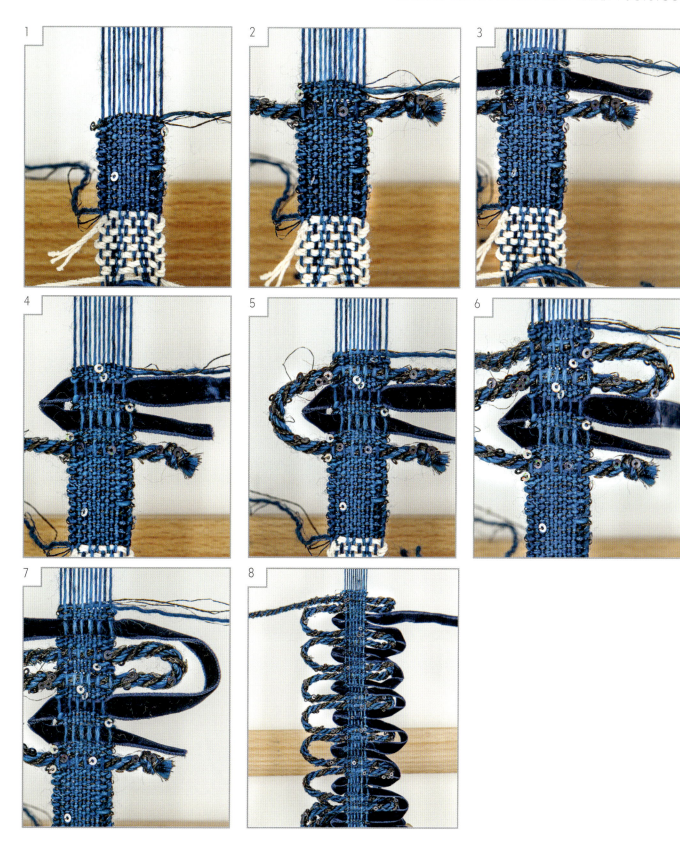

| 143

PROJECTS

STEP 2: FRINGE BUNCHES

PREPARATION
Weaving the fringe section for the Margot fringe for a footstool:

This fringe design uses an ingenious method for ensuring an even, straight-cut fringe. Two warps are used—one warp creates a header for the fringe, and a second, narrower warp holds the fringe in place while weaving. Once removed from the loom, this narrower warp is then cut off to reveal an even, straight, fringe.

1. Warp the loom with one warp of 12 warp ends.
2. Sley the reed, putting one warp end through each dent until eight warp ends are threaded through the reed. **(9)**
3. After the eighth warp end has been threaded, leave an empty gap in the reed of approximately 7 in. (17 cm). Sley the reed with the remaining four warp ends, putting one warp end through each dent.
4. Tie the warps securely to the front beam stick, making sure to keep the 7 in. (17 cm) gap between the warps. **(10)**
5. Weave the ground ends through both of the warps simultaneously. Weave ½ in. (1.2 cm) of plain weave, using SW on each warp separately. **(11)**
6. Weave a fringe bunch through both warps left to right. Weave one row of SW on each warp separately. **(12)**
7. Weave a fringe bunch through both warps right to left. Ensure that the fringe bunch does not pull on the right-hand warp. This warp must remain straight throughout the weaving process in order to achieve a consistent fringe length.
8. Weave one row of SW on each warp separately.
9. Repeat steps 6–9 until the desired length has been reached. **(13)**
10. Remove the fringe securely from the loom.

MARGOT CRÊTE FRINGE FOR A VELVET FOOTSTOOL

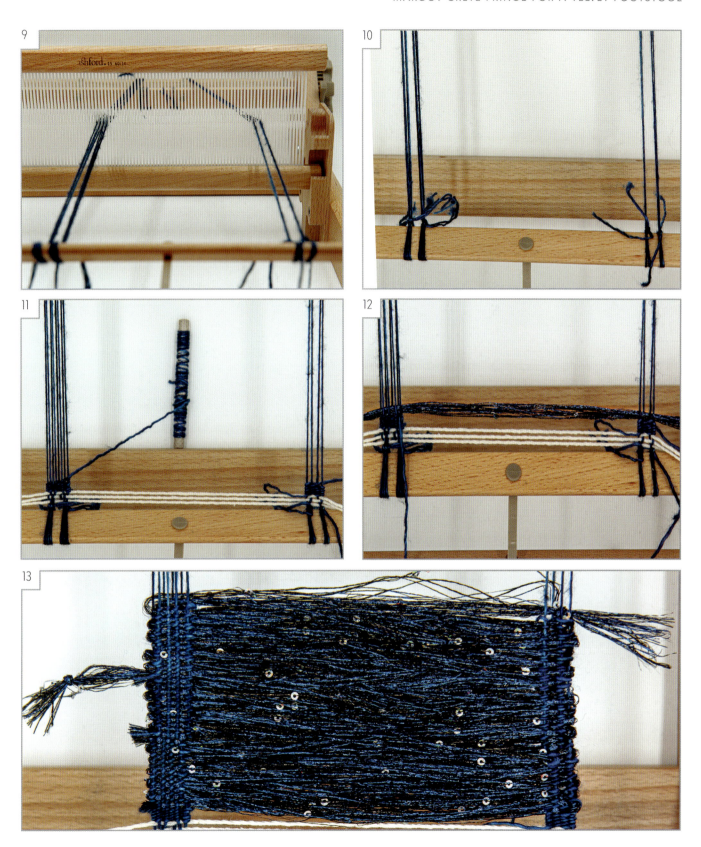

| 145

PROJECTS

CUTTING THE FRINGE

1. The fringe may look quite unruly when it is removed from the loom. Do not iron or steam synthetic yarn, as this can cause damage to the fibers. Gently shake and straighten the fringe. **(1)**
2. Lay the fringe vertically, right side up, on the table in front of you, with the narrower warp on the right-hand side.
3. Using a very sharp pair of scissors, cut through the middle of the narrow warp. Follow the warp up the length, cutting the design straight until the right-hand narrow warp is removed completely. **(2)**
4. Once the narrow warp is removed, you may need to trim off uneven fringe with a sharp pair of embroidery scissors.

JOINING THE HEADER AND FRINGE

1. Lay the fringe section down on a table horizontally.
2. Lay the crête header directly on top of the fringe, ensuring that the top warp ends line up. Gradually work down the length of the header and fringe, adjusting and pinning the two sections together. **(3)**
3. Using sewing thread and a sharps needle, join the two sections together with small stitches. You should need to join only the top two warp edges together down the entire length.

ATTACHING TO THE FOOTSTOOL

4. Lay the footstool flat on the tabletop, ensuring any joins in the upholstery are at the back of the footstool. Decide what height you want to apply your trim, so that the fringe hangs down nicely.
5. Measure the halfway point of the sewn trim lengths and place a pin through the trims to mark this point.
6. Locate the halfway point on the footstool. Line up the pinned halfway point of the trim with the halfway point of the footstool. Place a pin directly through the trims and footstool.
7. Work around the circumference of the footstool, pinning the trim down at 1 in. (2.5 cm) intervals. Check that the trims are being applied straight and level. **(4)**
8. Once pinned, use sewing thread and a regular sewing needle to attach the top edge of the trim to the footstool, using small, regular stitches.
9. I also spun a length of cord by using the same yarns that I used for the fringe. This cord is stitched along the seam between the footstool front and top, using a simple couching stitch.

MARGOT CRÊTE FRINGE FOR A VELVET FOOTSTOOL

1

2

3

4

| 147

CHROMATIC WAVES CURTAIN TIEBACK

This double crête design is a bold and colorful statement for your curtains. Woven using two warps that are linked through many interchanges between the decorative wefts, this design is fun to weave and beautiful to look at! The tieback is a little more complicated to weave because of the interchanges, but once you have woven a few repeats of the design, you will intuitively know which decorative weft to use next.

I've chosen a striking contrasting color palette for this design, which would sit well against block-color curtains. You could use any combination of colors and textures of decorative weft in order to pick out certain colors and shades from curtains you already own.

.

Equipment:

- Cord whipping: a wool needle and a extra length of MBW or a contrasting yarn.
- Material for guide strings (optional).
- Measuring tape.
- Pins.
- Rigid heddle loom.
- Scissors.
- Weaving bobbin or shuttle.
- Weights for guide strings (optional).
- 15 epi reed.

Materials and measurements

To make one tieback of 26 in. (66 cm) long × 5.5 in. (14 cm) wide:

- **Guide strings:** Optional.
- **Reed:** 15 epi reed, with one warp end per dent.
- **Warp yarn:** 100 percent wool, light/DK yarn. 2 oz. (50 g) is more than enough for warp and MBW.
- **Warp length:** 2 yd. (1.8 m).
- **Warp sett:** One warp of 16 ends, split into two warps of eight ends per warp, with a 1¼ in. (3 cm) gap in the reed between the warps.
- **Decorative wefts:** In total, 10 separate 60 in. (150 cm) lengths of DW are required. Each warp has its own set of decorative wefts (five per warp). Only five different DW are needed—this design uses the same materials on the right-hand warp and the left-hand warp.
- **Main body weft (MBW):** Same as warp. Two separate lengths of MBW are required—one to weave each warp.

PROJECTS

Calculating the length required for a curtain tieback:

1. Take the following measurements while your curtains are hung:
2. As a general rule of thumb, a curtain tieback is usually positioned one-third of the way up the curtain, measuring from the bottom of the curtain.
3. Scoop the curtain away from the window at the one-third point. Place a mark on the wall at that point.
4. Place the end of a tape measure over the one-third mark. Loop the tape measure around the gathered curtain at an angle, mimicking how a tieback would hold the curtain in place. Adjust the tape measure until you are happy with how the curtain is hanging.
5. Make a note of the total length of the tape measure.

Calculating the width required for a curtain tieback:

To a certain degree, the desired width of a tieback is a matter of taste. However, certain practical considerations must be taken into account, particularly the weight of the curtain fabric—if your curtains are heavy, the tieback will need to be wider to support the weight of the fabric.

General material tip: If your curtains are heavy, the yarns and cords used for weaving need to be able to support the weight of the curtain without losing the shape of the design. This weaving is going to be used horizontally on the curtain. As such, careful consideration is needed when selecting decorative weft materials. It is important to use decorative wefts that will not lose their shape or be bent out of alignment when attached to the curtain.

WARP SET UP

1. Warp the loom with a warp total of 16 ends.
2. Once the warp is wound onto the back beam, split the warp into two eight-end warps.
3. Sley the reed with the first warp of eight ends, placing one warp end per dent.
4. Leave a 1¼ in. (3 cm) gap in the reed to the right-hand side of the warp you have just sleyed.
5. Sley the reed with the second warp of eight ends, placing one warp end per dent.
6. Split the first warp bunch in half. Take four warp ends at a time and tie onto the front beam. Knot once. Repeat with the remaining four warp ends.
7. Repeat step 6 with the second warp, ensuring that the second warp is tied on approximately 1¼ in. (3 cm) away from the first warp.
8. The tension should be the same across both warps. Tighten or loosen the warps as needed. Knot the warp bunches again to secure.
9. Weave through the ground ends.

WEAVING

1. Weave 1 in. (2.5 cm) of plain weave on each warp separately, using MBW. **(1)**
2. Take one length of DW1. Weave DW1a right to left through the left-hand warp. Weave DW1b left to right through the right-hand warp. Change the shed and beat down well (ensure the shed is changed for each subsequent row). **(2)**
3. Weave two rows of MBW on each warp separately.
4. Take one length of DW2. Weave DW2a right to left through the left-hand warp. Weave the second length of DW2b left to right through the right-hand warp. **(3)**
5. Weave two rows of MBW on each warp separately.
6. Take one length of DW3. Weave DW3a right to left through the left-hand warp. Weave the second length of DW3b left to right through the right-hand warp. Weave two rows of MBW on each warp separately. **(4)**

CHROMATIC WAVES CURTAIN TIEBACK

PROJECTS

7. Repeat step 6 twice more, weaving DW4a and DW4b and DW5a and DW5a. (5)
8. All the DW on the left-hand warp should be facing left. All the DW on the right-hand warp should be facing right.
9. Starting on the left-hand warp: take DW5a and weave through the left-hand warp only, creating a very small picot on the left-hand side of the warp. Repeat the same process on the right-hand warp with DW5b. The picot will be on the right-hand side of the warp—a mirror image of the left-hand warp. Weave two rows MBW. (6)
10. Repeat step 9 with each of the remaining DW. Gradually the picots will become scallops on each warp edge. (7)
11. Weave DW1a right to left through the left-hand warp, creating a very small picot on the right-hand side. Weave DW1b left to right through the right-hand warp, creating a very small picot on the left-hand side. Weave two rows MBW. (8)
12. Weave DW2a right to left, creating a picot around DW1a. Weave DW2b left to right, creating a picot around DW1b. Weave two rows MBW. (9)
13. Repeat step 12 with DW3a and DW3b. Weave two rows MBW. (10)
14. Take DW5a (woven through the left-hand warp) across the gap between the two warps. Weave DW5a through the right-hand warp. The working length of DW5a will now be sitting on the right-hand side of the right-hand warp. (11)
15. Take DW5b (woven through the right-hand warp) across the gap between the two warps and underneath DW5a. Weave DW5b through the left-hand warp. The working length of DW5b will now be sitting on the left-hand side of the left-hand warp. Weave two rows MBW. DW5a and DW5b will be crossing over each other in the gap between the two warps. (12)
16. Repeat step 14 with DW4a. (13)

CHROMATIC WAVES CURTAIN TIEBACK

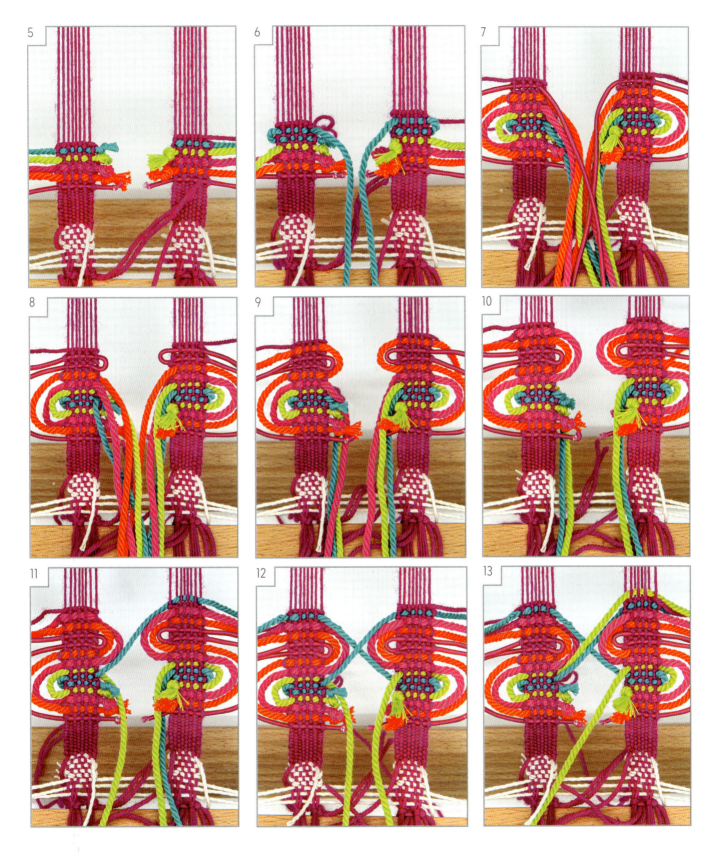

| 153

17. Repeat step 14 with DW4b. Weave two rows MBW. (14)
18. Weave DW4b left to right, creating a very small picot on the left-hand side of the left-hand warp. Weave DW4a right to left, creating a very small picot on the right-hand side of the right-hand warp. Weave two rows MBW.
19. Repeat step 19 with each of the DW until each DW has made a picot or a scallop on the outside edge of each warp. (15)
20. Continue to repeat the design until the desired length has been reached.
21. To finish, weave 1 in. (2.5 cm) of plain weave on each warp separately, using MBW.
22. Remove the weaving from the loom securely and finish ends, using your chosen method.

MAKING UP THE TIEBACK USING CORD WHIPPING

Cord whipping is a traditional technique that is used to create a secure yet decorative finished end for decorative wefts.

1. Lay the design flat on the table, with the right side up. Organize the decorative wefts into two distinct bunches and arrange them so that the DWs are sitting in order. (16)
2. Lay one DW bunch on top of the other DW bunch at a slight angle. (17)
3. Cut a length of yarn approx 12 in. (30 cm) long (either the same yarn as MBW or a contrast color, as shown here in blue), to be used as the whipping yarn. Fold this yarn in half. Place the loop of this yarn on top of the stacked DW bunches approximately 1.5 in. (3.8 cm) away from the warp ends. (18)
4. Place your thumb directly on top of the whipping-yarn loop. Open the lengths of whipping cord so they lie horizontal. (19)
5. Take the right-hand whipping-yarn length. Begin to tightly wrap this around the two fringe bunches. Wrap five times. (20, 21)
6. Remove your thumb. Thread the right-hand whipping-yarn length (that was used for wrapping) through the loop. (22)

CHROMATIC WAVES CURTAIN TIEBACK

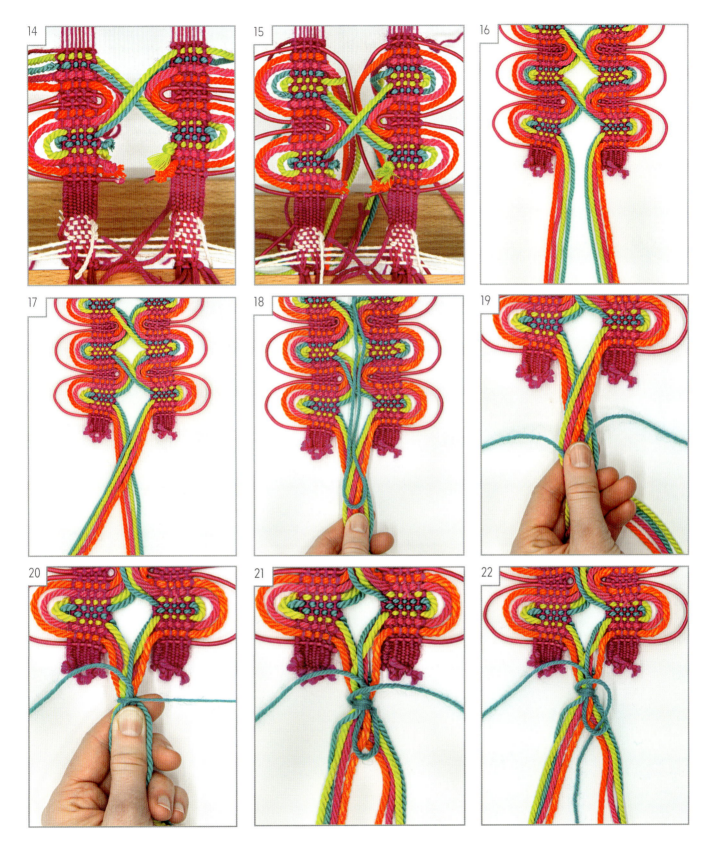

| 155

PROJECTS

7. Pull on both whipping-yarn lengths tightly to pull through both lengths. Don't yank these ends; pull them through methodically. **(23)**

8. Thread the top whipping-yarn length through a wool needle. Carefully pass the needle and yarn through the wrapped section from top to bottom. Repeat with the other yarn length, working from bottom to top. Trim both ends shorter. **(24)**

9. Repeat the cord-whipping process, adding a whipped section at roughly every 3 in. (7.5 cm) interval.* **(25)**

10. Repeat steps 1–10 with the other side of the tieback.

*Depending on the chosen length of your tieback.

GLOSSARY

braid: Yarns that have been interlaced to create a three-dimensional cord, rope, or tube. Braid can sometimes be used to create a hollow tube.

beater: Used to compress/"beat down" the weft yarn rows as the weaving progresses.

beading needle: A very fine needle with a small eye, used for passing thread through beads.

cord: A set of yarns that have been spun together to form a thicker cord. Cord is used extensively to create scallops and picots.

cord whipping: A decorative technique used to secure the ends of a cord or braid.

crête: Literal translation of the French is ridge or crest. Crête makes a ribbed or ridged effect.

decorative weft (DW): Decorative weft is the yarn, cord, braid, material, etc. used to create the scallops and picots in a design.

dent: General term for an open space in the reed.

dressing the loom: Setting up the loom for weaving. Steps include warp making, warp winding, sleying the reed, and tying on.

end: One individual warp thread.

ends per inch (EPI, epi): Unit of textile measurement. The number of warp ends needed per inch of woven fabric.

eyes: An opening that looks like a large eye of a needle in the reed. Specific to reeds made for rigid heddle looms. One warp yarn at a time is threaded through an eye.

four-hook cord spinner: A handheld device that spins individual yarns into a cord.

fringe posts: Two points that yarn can be wrapped around in order to create a bunch of fringe.

gimp: A traditional passementerie material made from a core yarn, or often wire, that has been tightly wrapped with another yarn to create a material that holds its shape when weaving scallop and picot.

ground ends: The three initial rows of weaving that are woven through the warp at the beginning of every project. Woven using strong weft yarn, the guide strings are looped and tied to the front beam stick under tension while being woven through the warp.

guide string: A technique for weaving consistently sized scallops and picots. Strong lengths of yarn that sit next to the warp selvages.

hank of yarn: A continuous loop of yarn.

joining in weft: When a length of MBW runs out, a new length of MBW is joined into the weaving.

main body weft yarn (MBW): Weft yarn that creates the solid areas of plain weave.

picot: A smaller decorative loop that is formed along the selvages. There is no prescribed size for a picot. However, when both small loops and larger loops exist within the same design, the smaller loop is always referred to as a scallop.

plain weave: A woven structure. This simplest of all woven structures, plain weave (often called "tabby") works by interlacing the warp yarn with the weft yarn in a one-under, one-over construction.

plied yarn: One yarn made from combining multiple strands of yarn together.

quill: *See* bobbin.

reed hook: A flat hook used to pull the warp yarns through the dents in the reed.

reed: Either made from metal or a combination of wood and plastic (depending on the type of loom the reed is made for). Has a series of openings across the width of the reed that act as a comb, used to both separate and hold the warp yarn evenly across the width of the warp. Also acts as the beater. A reed made for a rigid heddle loom has eyes and slots. A variety of different-sized reeds are available, depending on the specifics of the project being woven.

rigid heddle: *See* reed.

scallop: A larger decorative loop that is formed along the selvages. There is no prescribed size for a scallop. However, when both small loops and larger loops exist within the same design, the larger loop is always referred to as a scallop.

selvage: The left-hand side and the right-hand side edges of the woven fabric.

sett: The number of ends per inch in the warp. The sett determines the density of the finished woven fabric.

shed: The shed is the open space between the raised and lowered warp threads through which the weft passes. The shed is created by raising or lowering the warp through raising or lowering the reed.

shuttle: Used to hold and carry the weft yarn through the shed. The most common types of shuttle are a boat shuttle and a stick shuttle, both available in various lengths.

sleying the reed: The action of pulling the warp yarns through the reed with a reed hook.

slots: A long vertical opening in the reed, specifically to reeds made for rigid heddle looms. One warp yarn at a time is threaded through a slot.

RESOURCES AND SUPPLIERS

structural weft: An additional weft yarn that creates stability within the selvages when weaving passementerie designs, such as fringes.

take-up: The natural warp shrinkage that occurs when the finished length is removed from the tension of the loom.

tapestry needle: *See* **wool needle.**

warp: The vertical yarns that are held under tension on the loom. The warp is the foundation of weaving. *See* **end.**

warp-faced weaving: Fabric that has many more warp threads than weft threads on the surface of the textile. No weft can be seen through the warp.

weaving bobbin: Usually a hollow tube made from thick cardboard, or wood. Used to hold the weft yarn inside a shuttle.

weaving in weft tails/ends: Once the weaving is removed from the loom, the weft tails are woven into the back of the woven textile, using a wool/tapestry needle.

weft: The horizontal yarns that interchange with the warp in order to create woven fabric. The weft weaves horizontally from selvage to selvage.

weft-faced weaving: Fabric that has many more weft threads than warp threads on the surface of the textile.

weft tail: 6 in. (15 cm) length of MBW yarn that is left dangling from the selvage when the weaving is started and ended. Weft tails are also left when joining in weft midweaving.

wool needle: A blunt needle with a large eye. Available in a range of lengths.

RESOURCES AND SUPPLIERS

For each project I made a particular point of purchasing yarns and materials from small, independent companies. I encourage you to look at these resources listed below, but also to make a point of sourcing materials from independent suppliers that are local to you. Individual stores often have an exciting range of hand-dyed yarns and interesting materials to choose from.

Creating passementerie can also be an ideal craft for using yarn and materials that you may already have in your stash.

Yarn

AMO Yarn
DMC
La Bien Aimée
Loop London
Madeline Tosh
Orchidean Luxury Fibers—hand-dyed yarn to order
Qing Fiber

Rowan Yarns
Tribe Yarns
West Yorkshire Spinners
Wool & the Gang
Wool Warehouse
Yarn on a Cone
Yarns to Yearn For

Haberdashery, decorative weft, and traditional gimp cord suppliers

DMC—traditional gimp cord supplier (North America only)
Gina-B Silkworks—traditional gimp cord supplier
Mac Culloch & Wallis
New Trimmings
Plum Bowtique

Equipment and tools

Anna Crutchley cord winder
Handweavers Shop and Gallery
Ashford—Rigid heddle looms, large frame looms, and other weaving equipment

ACKNOWLEDGMENTS

Thank you to my loving husband and parents for their unwavering support throughout this incredible journey of writing and completing my book. Without their love, encouragement, and understanding, this book would not have been possible. To my husband, Stephen, and to my parents, Carol and David, this book is dedicated to you.

Stephen, thank you for embracing the idiosyncrasies of being married to an artist so wholeheartedly. You have been my rock throughout this process, inspiring me to chase my dreams and providing the necessary guidance and reassurance when self-doubt crept in. Thank you for your endless patience and understanding. Your sense of adventure, your willingness to try new things, and your zest for life inspire me every day to embrace life with enthusiasm. Thank you, my darling. I love you. TAP.

Thank you to my parents, Carol and David, for always believing in me. I am so lucky to have such remarkable parents who have always stood by my side. Your constant belief in my abilities has propelled me forward, and your unwavering encouragement and support have pushed me to dream big and to follow my passions. Thank you—I love you.

Dad, thank you for passing on your creative gene to me and thank you for setting a great example of using creativity to craft a successful career. You seamlessly made the switch from sports photographer to passementerie photographer, enthusiastically and selflessly embracing your new role. Thank you for your kindness, patience, hard work, and expertise while photographing all the step-by-step projects.

Mum, I vividly remember the first contemporary art exhibition we saw together, and ever since that day you have been with me on this journey. Your unconditional love and support has been a constant source of strength, providing me with the confidence to pursue my dreams and conquer any obstacles that come my way. You have always believed in me, even when I doubted myself, and that belief has been instrumental in my successes. Your sacrifices and selflessness have never gone unnoticed, and I am eternally grateful for all that you have done for me. Thank you.

Thank you to Jo and the team at BlueRed Press for your patience, hard work, and advocacy of this amazing, endangered craft.

ABOUT THE AUTHOR

(Photo: Jeff Gilbert, 2023)

Elizabeth Ashdown, one of only a few professional passementerie artists working in the UK today, has been credited with reinvigorating this endangered heritage craft. She combines the centuries-old skills with a contemporary aesthetic to create acclaimed artworks. She is a graduate of the Royal College of Art and of Central Saint Martins. Working from her studio in London, Elizabeth creates passementerie for a diverse range of clients, from commissions for private collectors to custom lengths of passementerie for interior designers. Elizabeth also teaches the craft of passementerie through her master classes. Her work has been featured in publications such as *Embroidery Magazine*, *Pom Pom Quarterly*, *Crafts Magazine*, *The Textile Eye*, *Selvedge*, *Living Etc*, and *Homes & Gardens*. Her studio is in London, UK. | www.elizabethashdown.co.uk